SUPER
CROSSWORDS

SUPER CROSSWORDS

OVER
150
PUZZLES

This edition published in 2021 by Arcturus Publishing Limited
26/27 Bickels Yard, 151–153 Bermondsey Street,
London SE1 3HA

AD010147US

Printed in the UK

1

Across

1. Animal with two feet
6. "Carmina Burana" composer Carl
10. Alpine feeder
11. Country great Haggard
13. Association
15. Comcast and NetZero, e.g.
16. P.T.A. interest, briefly
17. Shogun's capital
19. Dummy
21. Garden product word
22. Sound recording
25. French W.W. I soldier
26. Flat, simple boats
29. Large and important church
31. Final: abbr.
33. Appearance-challenged woman
34. "…all that wealth ___ gave": Gray
35. It's bought by the bar
37. Amble
39. They're awarded annually on December 10th: 2 wds.
43. "Duino Elegies" poet
44. Brain passages
45. Wide widths, initially
46. 200 precious milligrams

Down

1. Pen or lighter brand
2. Bar opener?
3. Arrangement of chemical elements by atomic number: 2 wds.
4. Misdials, e.g.
5. Georgia, Alabama, Louisiana, etc.: 2 wds.
6. Grandma: Ger.
7. Network of blood vessels or nerves
8. Kitchen appliance: hyph.
9. Bread ingredient
12. Old ExxonMobil brand name
14. Aspiring atty.'s exam
17. Literary monogram
18. Electronic act Justice, e.g.
20. One-time widely-used pain reliever
23. Dockworkers' gp.
24. Walk softly
27. ___ kwon do
28. Camera inits.
30. Angelic instrument
31. Mil. backup group
32. He outranks the sarge
36. "Lion dog," briefly
38. Ars longa, ___ brevis
40. "___ Liaisons Dangereuses"
41. It's full of periods
42. Mach 1 breaker, initially

2

Across

1 Long-range weapon, briefly
5 Animals
10 Daughter of Zeus and Demeter in Greek mythology
11 Dressed (up)
12 Month before Nisan
13 Channeled
14 Brewer's kiln
15 Boston's Liberty Tree, e.g.
16 Caspian and Caribbean
18 Not yet final, at law
22 Accomplishments
24 Rock band equipment
25 "___ got a golden ticket…"
26 Air hero
28 Fraternity members
29 Give or take, e.g.
31 Bug
33 Length x width, for a rectangle
34 Cattail, e.g.
35 ___ de Triomphe
37 Baby-talk characteristic
40 Kind of number
43 Animal shelter
44 Right, in a way
45 Volcano in Verne's "Journey to the Center of the Earth"
46 It can give a golfer a lift
47 Take five, say

Down

1 Aviation org.
2 Closing passage
3 Woman's garment
4 Sable kin
5 April honoree
6 Barnard graduate, e.g.
7 Final: abbr.
8 French word in wedding announcements
9 Continue
11 Formal theater area: 2 wds.
17 Ottoman officer
19 Straightaway
20 Blueprint item, briefly
21 "___ It Romantic?"
22 Prima donna
23 Frequent word from ham operators
27 Opposite WSW
30 Giving a bleat
32 Buyer's counterpart
36 ___ Against the Machine (rock-rap group)
38 Breaks a commandment
39 Duff
40 Cutter
41 Party time, maybe
42 Cabernet color

3

Across

1. Level, in London
5. Broadway opening?: 2 wds.
11. "... a bug in ___": 2 wds.
12. Jimmy Stewart played one in "Rear Window"
13. Actress Diana
14. Prepares to transplant
15. Biblical mother of Jabal and Jubal
16. T-shirt label abbr.
17. Roger in "Nicholas Nickelby"
19. OPEC meas.
23. Takes it easy
26. Contents of some barrels
27. Make smaller, in a way
28. His real name was Arthur
30. Foreign dignitary
31. "Be sensible": 2 wds.
33. Internet guffaw
35. U2's "___ of Homecoming"
36. Age abbr.
38. Kansas city on the Neosho River
41. Third generation Japanese-American
44. Chemical ending
45. Scarpered: 2 wds.
46. Artificial bait
47. Small sheepdog, familiarly
48. Dagger

Down

1. Singular, to Caesar
2. Desertlike
3. Rio de Janeiro's ___ Mountain: 2 wds.
4. Brainiac
5. Pull or pluck off
6. D.C. gp.
7. Laid-back: 2 wds.
8. Antipoverty agcy. created by LBJ
9. Crackpot
10. Hospital sections, initially
18. Big boss, for short
20. Springsteen hit: 3 wds.
21. T'ang dynasty poet
22. At a snail's pace
23. Behind
24. Cogito-sum connector
25. Doofus: var.
29. Overhead photos
32. Harden
34. Janitor's supply
37. Broken, old-style
39. Harp's cousin
40. Hard direction
41. Grads-to-be, for short
42. "That's relaxing!"
43. SSW's reverse

4

Across

1 Garment parts

8 "No use arguing with me": 2 wds.

9 Wall St. action

12 Fraudulent appropriation of funds

14 Do it wrong

15 Blissful

16 Comes (to)

19 Pollster's detection

20 Put into effect, as a law

22 Types of newsgroups, initially

23 Grasshopper's cousin

25 Haunting sound

27 Heaps

29 Train tracks

31 "___ (Understands)". Tammy Wynette song: 2 wds.

33 Distresses

35 By way of

36 Awkward situation

39 Prescription instruction, initially

40 Artist's paint-mixing board

41 Absorb the attention of

Down

1 Teams

2 Reinforcing rib used in Gothic vaulting

3 Given the right to vote

4 Tikkanen of the N.H.L.

5 Cruella de ___, 101 Dalmatians antagonist

6 Ending for effer or fluor

7 City in Germany

9 President's selective rejection: hyph., 2 wds.

10 Sound of a bounce

11 How some songs are sold: 2 wds.

13 In an curt manner

17 Released conditionally

18 "Nova" subj.

21 ___/IP

24 Actress Basinger

25 Blow one's top

26 Resort island off the coast of Italy

28 People of exceptional holiness

30 Michael of R.E.M.

32 Archibald and Thurmond of the NBA Hall of Fame

34 Diagnostic test

37 N. Afr. country

38 Mal de ___ (seasickness)

5

Across

1. ____-loading (pre-marathon activity)
6. Chuck
10. TV soldiers of fortune: hyph.
11. Below-the-belt
12. Darn it!
14. "Wheel of Fortune" buy: 2 wds.
15. "Fancy that!"
16. Yoko born in Tokyo
17. Ofc. computer link
18. "We ____ to please"
19. Certain digital watch face, for short
20. Bed board
22. Pried
24. Failed to be
26. Muzzle
28. Primordial matter, to physicists
32. Aegean, Red or Adriatic, e.g.
33. Bachelor's home
35. Popeye's "Positively!"
36. Body part that also means "cool"
37. Absorbed, as a cost
38. Big Apple attraction, with "The"
39. Not removable (of a right)
42. Like some consonant sounds
43. Down producer
44. ____ brat
45. Bugle sounds

Down

1. Intrigues
2. Hard on the ear, maybe
3. Focal point
4. "____ humbug!" (Scrooge's shout)
5. 1980s Olds clone of Chevrolet Citation
6. Black-throated ____ (Asian bird)
7. Black, white and orange bird
8. Blotto
9. Church assembly
11. Evil spirit: var.
13. Restore control, say
21. "____ Buck Chuck" (Charles Shaw)
23. Chester White's home
25. Domestic: 2 wds.
26. Fisherman with a net
27. Flamethrower fuel
29. Greek consonant
30. Button holder
31. Gauges
32. Hindu deity
34. Star in Cygnus
40. Produce, as an egg
41. Have what's "going around"

6

Across

1 Front of a manuscript leaf
6 Novi Sad residents
11 Busybody
12 Heavy water, for one
13 South African grassland
14 Inlay on some guitars
15 ___ Lane (Clark Kent co-worker)
17 N.Y.C. cultural institution
18 Springsteen's "Born in the ___"
20 Thus, in Turin
22 Certain student, for short
24 French candy
28 Spanish houses
30 Helmsley of hotels
31 Became an adult: 2 wds.
33 Batters' stats
34 Heavy, durable furniture wood
36 Hamilton's prov.
37 Trig. function
40 Substitute: abbr.
42 Gp.
44 Complete taxing work online?: hyph.
47 Cook, as beans
48 Fencing move
49 Chess pieces
50 "Holy cow!"

Down

1 Bible edition, initially
2 Hydrocarbon suffix
3 Fall down, as in a heap
4 Brouhaha: hyph.
5 Eye-related
6 Trinity component
7 Adjudicator, questioner
8 "Little Caesar" role
9 Real estate ad abbr.
10 "I ___ Dark Stranger" (1946 movie): 2 wds.
16 Blubber
18 Homeland Security org.
19 Go paragliding, say
21 La lead-in
23 Shrub also called may
25 Meadowlark relative
26 "Bring It ___ It to Win It" (2007 movie starring Ashley Benson): 2 wds.
27 Big name in magazine publishing
29 Challenge, legally
32 Five, for some golf holes
35 Conrad ___, "Original Machines" singer
37 Ball field covering
38 Floating, perhaps
39 "Don't let your boss catch you watching this" initials
41 "Bah, humbug!"
43 Baseball great Young et al.
45 Big: abbr.
46 Suffix meaning "recipients of an action"

7

Across

1 "The Mary Tyler Moore Show" spinoff
6 Russian pop duo
10 Canvas supporter
11 Ken and Lena
13 Song on "Beatles for Sale": 2 wds.
15 Ceremony words: 2 wds.
16 It's like -like
17 Express regret
18 "Sisters" costar: 2 wds.
20 "___: Deadliest Roads" (reality TV series)
21 Criteria: abbr.
22 Raises a glass to
24 "Battling Bella" of 1970s politics
26 Abbr. in a letter salutation before multiple surnames
29 Butts
33 Actress Gardner
34 Pastoral poem
36 "Sure," slangily
37 Sounds of doubt
38 Tampa to Jacksonville dir.
39 It may give you more sleep: 2 wds.
42 To the point
43 From head ___ (completely): 2 wds.
44 Brit. decorations
45 Go too fast

Down

1 Pays
2 "You know how ___ can be" (Beatles line): 2 wds.
3 1970s teen idol Donny
4 In excelsis ___
5 Cool
6 "I ___ So" (Randy Travis song): 2 wds.
7 Muhammad ___ (boxing great)
8 River that flows through Baghdad
9 Not injured
12 Restores to copy
14 Philosopher Friedrich
19 Gray and Candler
23 Earthy prefix
25 Light winds
26 "That time of year thou ___ in me behold" (Shakespeare's Sonnet 73)
27 Made square
28 Matters of taste
30 Descended from the same male ancestor
31 ___ Tavern, Revolutionary War site in Massachusetts
32 Felt
35 Exams for future attys.
40 Bear, in Spain
41 Slice (off)

8

Across

1. Financial newspaper, for short
4. Special effects used in "Avatar," e.g.
7. Fair hiring letters, for short
8. ____ Magnon
9. Chest muscle, for short
12. Aboveboard
14. Make bigger, like a photo: abbr.
15. Algae bed?
16. Fatherland, to Flavius
18. Do away with
20. Those things, in Tijuana
21. ____ Stadium (D.C. United's home)
22. Flightless bird
24. Stores
26. Georgia O'Keeffe Museum city: 2 wds.
28. FDR home loan org.
31. Put up, as a picture
32. Crams
34. "In ____ and out the other": 2 wds.
36. Archeology venue, at times
37. Make sense, with "up"
38. "It's Too Late Now" autobiographer: 3 wds.
40. Scottish novelist Josephine
41. Broke bread
42. A limited number of
43. Sound of satisfaction

Down

1. Niobe, e.g.
2. Start a trip: 2 wds.
3. 35th President: 3 wds.
4. New Deal agcy.
5. Henry Fonda film of 1940, with "The": 3 wds.
6. Seat of Allen County, Kan.
9. Arm of the Arabian Sea: 2 wds.
10. Early supercomputer
11. Conflict
13. "High Sierra" actress Lupino
17. Austin of "Knots Landing"
19. Barry Manilow song locale
23. Certain surgeon's "patient"
25. Homeowner's regular pymt.
26. Young hog
27. "Biography" network: 3 wds.
29. "Die Lorelei" poet
30. Good ____: 2 wds.
33. Soft & ____ (Gillette brand)
35. Battery for small devices, initially
39. "I'm not real impressed"

9

Across

1 Brit's service discharge
6 Apt rhyme for "stash"
11 Actor Vincent of "Alphabet City"
12 Having a lot to lose?
13 Eldest Griffin child in "Family Guy"
14 Fragrant rootstock used in perfumes
15 China's Sun Yat-___
16 "Sesame Street" Muppet
18 Mathematician who is the subject of the book "The Man Who Loved Only Numbers"
20 Cooler
23 Time still to come
25 Take it for a slide, outside
26 Accord
27 Cut drastically, as prices
28 "___ Ado About Nothing"
29 Mammals of the weasel family
30 "Unbelievable" band of 1991
31 Bizarre
32 ___ probability (near-certain): 2 wds.
34 "Mamma ___" (ABBA song)
37 Say "not guilty," for example
39 Hibernation holes
41 Assured
42 Acclamation
43 "Alas …"
44 Census ___

Down

1 Prestigious mil. awards
2 Fencer's blade
3 It's described by the dynamo theory: 2 wds.
4 ___ roll (doing well): 2 wds.
5 Completely devoid of water: hyph.
6 Masked creatures, briefly
7 Dugout shelter
8 Breakfast for some: 3 wds.
9 Chu-___ (legendary Confucian sage)
10 Some M.I.T. grads
17 Fishy eggs
19 Baby ___ (candy bar)
21 Roll-top, for one
22 Old English letters
23 Feel vexation
24 "One" on a one
25 Cast aspersions on
27 Frying pan
29 Partner of poivre
31 Australian Aboriginal's war club
33 Hammer's target
35 Wrath, in Latin hymns
36 Heavenly subj.?
37 Ltr. additions
38 Hawaii's Mauna ___
40 Code breakers' org.

Across

1. Buffalo hockey player
6. Ginger cookies
11. More unwell
12. Apocryphal Old Testament book
13. La ___, Argentinian port
14. Daughter of Juan Carlos I
15. Financial security: 2 wds.
17. Drudges
18. Bull fight matador
21. "Did You Ever ___ Lassie?": 2 wds.
25. Feeling blue
26. Letters on a Cardinal's cap
28. Hemingway's "The Old Man and the ___"
29. Blog feeds, initially
31. Living room piece
33. Ralph of "The Waltons"
35. Machine replacement pieces: 2 wds.
40. Game with numbered balls
41. Helvetica alternative
42. Clinging plants
43. Wedge-shaped bones
44. "Fiddle-___!": 2 wds.
45. Expressionless

Down

1. Onetime football quarterback Brian
2. "It was ___ huge mistake!": 2 wds.
3. "Gil ___" (Alain-René Lesage novel)
4. Enter again, as data
5. Back-to-school purchases
6. Area to the rear
7. At least: 2 wds.
8. As busy as ___: 2 wds.
9. Blood-donation amount
10. Railroad stop: abbr.
16. Hoffman movie of 1982
18. Dungeons & Dragons game co., initially
19. Grp. founded in Bogotá
20. Ave. cousins
22. Extreme ending
23. Shoebox letters
24. Tooth-doctors' org.
27. Allow to overtake: 2 wds.
30. "Way down upon the ___ River…"
32. Attack: 2 wds.
34. Appeared
35. Golfer Ballesteros
36. Handed over money
37. "Little Caesar" role
38. Mountain pool
39. Kill, in the Bible
40. Signal at auction

11

Across

1. Lobster eater's garb, for some reason
4. Not lamented or mourned for
10. Kind of newspaper page: hyph.
12. Without an owner: 2 wds.
13. Skeleton part, in Padua
14. Go for
15. Capital of Mozambique
17. Rocket stage
19. Derek and Jackson
22. In secret: 3 wds.
24. "Barely Lethal" studio, initially
25. Up to me: 3 wds.
27. Dr. ___
28. Be unhappy: 2 wds.
29. Either end of a wide grin
30. German women
31. "Relax, soldier!": 2 wds.
34. Bathing, probably: 3 wds.
39. Dies ___
40. Official
41. Bismarck's state: abbr., 2 wds.
42. Approve of
43. G.R.E. takers

Down

1. Sound of thunder
2. Res ___ loquitur (law)
3. Sprinkle with mud, etc.
4. Not able to be defeated
5. Classic Japanese drama
6. Go a-courting
7. Coldplay's "Viva la Vida" producer Brian
8. Zoologist's foot
9. Mao ___-tung
11. Soft and sticky
16. Irritate: 2 wds.
18. Soft drinks brand of Pennsylvania: hyph.
19. Uniform armbands
20. Tex. neighbor
21. Auction cry
22. French wave
23. "A Doll's House" wife
26. Inform: 2 wds.
32. Coal-rich German region
33. Comic cries
34. "___ job's worth doing…": 2 wds.
35. Silent assent
36. Supply with weapons
37. "Don't tell me any more!," initially
38. Defunct org. that included Syria, initially

12

Across

1 Susan of "All My Children"
6 Beloved
10 Depth charge targets: hyph.
12 Easily maneuverable, as a ship
13 Mickey Mouse's mate
14 Feudal worker
15 Mideast capital: var.
16 Lean-___ (sheds)
17 China's Sun ___-sen
19 C.S. Lewis's lion
22 Got gray
24 King of pop
27 Famed Russian cosmonaut: 2 wds.
29 Strappy shoe
30 Geographical features, for short
31 Grocery section
33 "Some ___ meat and canna eat": Burns
34 Deli order, initially
36 Siouan tribe
38 Eye, to Pierre
40 Timber resembling rosewood
43 Tire (out)
44 Sonora snooze
45 Ireland's ___ Fein
46 Advance toward night

Down

1 Erstwhile radio duo, ___ and Abner
2 Where, in Latin
3 Anxiety and confusion
4 First miracle site
5 Turner autobiography: 2 wds.
6 Coloring fluid
7 Compass point at 67.5 degrees: hyph.
8 Florence is on it
9 Roger of "Cheers"
11 Edible marine bivalves: 2 wds.
17 Childish cheers
18 Lago contents
20 Lose minutes
21 Composer Khachaturian
23 Stu's wife on "Rugrats"
25 "Swept Away" director Wertmüller
26 Massachusetts motto opener
28 Neon, e.g.
32 Dot-com commerce: hyph.
34 Knocks on the head
35 Sainted pope called "the Great": 2 wds.
37 Concert halls
39 Hosp. employee, perhaps
41 Western native
42 Kal ___ (pet food brand)

13

Across

1 Walk proudly

6 Desire desperately

11 Rushing sound: var.

12 Confine: 2 wds.

13 External

14 Waugh and Guinness

15 Foreordain

17 Home of the brave

18 ___ Bell (fast food chain)

21 Clumsy

25 Caribbean music

26 Oxlike beast

27 Cote quote

28 Compassion

30 Strip of leather

31 Be sweet on

33 Sensor that reads a bar code: 2 wds.

38 Throng

39 Battery part

40 Old Dodge

41 Hopping mad

42 Denim pants

43 Shakes hands with

Down

1 Switch: var.

2 ___ de force

3 Mechanical repetition

4 In the habit of: 2 wds.

5 Babe Ruth's number

6 French castle

7 Alleviation

8 Sermon signoff

9 "Miami ___" (crime drama series)

10 Print measures

16 Benefactor

18 Cooking meas.

19 Alias, initially

20 Meowing pet

22 ___ cream sundae

23 Staff note

24 Steamy

26 Vesta or Venus

29 Go solid

30 ___ Babies (popular dolls)

32 Area of influence

33 Nuclear reactor section

34 Diva's big moment

35 Antiwar advocate

36 Do some cutting, maybe

37 1981 Warren Beatty movie about communism

38 Leon Uris novel, with "The"

14

Across

1 Pole on a ship

5 Shining

11 Elbe tributary

12 Area around the goal in ice hockey (with "the")

13 Lyndon Johnson's younger daughter

14 Physical well-being

15 Potter

17 Robert ____: 2 wds.

18 Low's opposite

22 Suffix with respond

24 Talk show host Hall

26 Thirst

28 Papal vestment

29 Remedy for any ailment: hyph.

31 Former Mideast inits.

32 Florida archipelago

33 Like diehard fans

35 Game show competitor

39 Removing

42 Letter-shaped girder: hyph.

43 Chinese philosopher of long ago: hyph.

44 "The Aviator" actor Alan

45 Trade

46 Poor marks

Down

1 Nickname of the Spice Girls' Sporty Spice: 2 wds.

2 Malaria symptom

3 Government dept. V.I.P.

4 Courtroom proceeding

5 More sore

6 College srs. may sit for them

7 Tanned animal skin

8 Suffix with arbor or app

9 Bermuda clock setting, initially

10 "Whatever" grunt

16 "It don't ____ thing if it ain't got that swing": 2 wds.

19 Not able to be heard

20 ____ monster

21 Field worker

22 Flemish painter Jan van ____

23 ____ Galerie (Manhattan art museum)

25 Work out

27 Postponement

30 German golfer Bernhard

34 Homeric epic

36 Handle, in France

37 "Smooth Operator" singer

38 Refrain syllables

39 RN's knack

40 "____ approved" (motel sign)

41 S. ____ (Seoul's country: abbr.)

15

Across

1 Evelyn ____, "Brideshead Revisited" writer
6 Captures via VCR
11 Breathing problem
12 Said rude words
13 Drinker's accident
14 Chubby
15 Two-seater
17 Agitation
18 "The Lord of the Rings" figure
19 Orange tuber
21 Genetic material, initially
22 Grubby guy
24 Loafer doodad
26 Knock: hyph.
28 Musket accessory
30 Guinea pigs, maybe
33 Historical period, or a detergent brand
34 Elephant's weight, maybe
36 Character used in density
37 "Hamlet" has five
39 ____ coaster
41 Posts
43 Bring up, as a child
44 Brief stanza
45 Cooper cars
46 Oceanic abysses
47 Anxiety

Down

1 Doesn't use
2 Horrify
3 Giving few or no details
4 Money: Ger.
5 "Roots" writer
6 Prescribed amt., sometimes
7 Bookbinder's tools
8 Brit. currency: 2 wds.
9 Fine fur
10 Of a partition
16 One who accepts charges?
20 "Welcome" site?
23 Place for a drink
25 Drain, as someone's energy
27 "Sesame Street" watcher
28 Didn't just criticize
29 Esoteric
31 Argument
32 Most mad
35 Actress Shearer
38 Food for pigs
40 (Had) reclined
42 Certain sibling, slangily

16

Across

1. Full range
6. "Do I ___ to eat a peach?": T.S. Eliot
10. Less than 90 degrees, as an angle
11. Grande ___ (La Sorbonne, e.g.)
13. "Chill!"
14. Utah's ___ Canyon
15. Oscilloscope part, initially
16. Drs.' group
18. Feel fluish
19. Japanese sash
20. Dil Pickles's dad on "Rugrats"
21. The Mormon Church, in initials
22. Boy, to his madre
24. Pituitary hormone, initially
26. Math subj.
28. Prince, e.g.
30. Peter, for one
32. Non-profit, voluntary citizens' groups, initially
34. Kind of particle
36. The Chesapeake, e.g.
38. Ad ___
39. "Hold On Tight" band, to fans
40. "Son ___ gun!": 2 wds.
41. Like one in a series
42. "Book 'em, ___!" (Hawaii Five-O catchphrase)
44. Overcome utterly
46. Several Russian tsars
47. Leisurely stroll
48. Part of a C.S.A. signature: 2 wds.
49. Networks: abbr.

Down

1. French waiter
2. Biting
3. Involving several countries
4. Hagen of "Reversal of Fortune"
5. State, capital Austin
6. Corrupt
7. Not down: abbr.
8. Regal title: 2 wds.
9. Charlton Heston title role: 2 wds.
12. Congers
17. Underground letters
23. They protect QBs
25. Midmorning
27. Freight unit
29. Rhizoid
31. W.W. II inits.
33. Dummies
34. Prefix with cab
35. Drudge
37. Talks foolishly or noisily
43. Weather vane dir., sometimes
45. Fodder

17

Across

1 Greek portico
5 Coffin-carrying car
11 Charged particles
12 Flunky: hyph.
13 Racecar servicing areas
14 Searched for water
15 K-12, in education: hyph.
16 Big TV maker
17 Boston Bruins Line
19 At no time, poetically
23 Covets
26 Big D.C. lobby letters
27 ___ Amin, former dictator of Uganda
28 Bullring "Bravo!"
29 Largest city in Mich.
30 Abet
31 Most cheeky
33 Hair removal brand
35 Actor Michael of "Year One"
36 D.C. summer clock setting
38 Hertz competitor
41 Non-scary ghost
44 Bit
45 Noble Italian family name
46 "Star Trek" counselor, Deanna
47 Bitter tasting
48 IRS IDs

Down

1 Thin slit in a tire tread
2 Trouble's partner, in Shakespeare
3 Served separately from the main dish: 3 wds.
4 Birthplace of a saint
5 Like some dams
6 Anti-discrimination group, initially
7 It's upstream from Luxor
8 Apt. ad info
9 Manuscript encl.
10 Discontinue
18 Support, with "up"
20 Tries hard
21 "___ tú" it's you, in Spain
22 "Infestation" rock group
23 Anthropologist Fossey
24 Adams of "Up in Smoke"
25 All dried up
32 Distinguishing characteristics
34 Lukewarm
37 Prefix meaning one tenth
39 Lay ___ the line (gamble): 2 wds.
40 "Je ne ___ quoi"
41 Nashville-based awards org.
42 N.R.C. predecessor
43 "Star Wars" project of the 1980s

18

Across

1 Attired
5 Pirate costume part
11 Apiary feature
12 ___ borealis
13 Bypass
14 "Two ___ don't make a right"
15 Temporary insurance certificates: 2 wds.
17 Hope or community follower
18 "___ through the tulips"
21 Fall gemstone
25 High card, in many games
26 Eggs, to a biologist
27 Grizzly, e.g.
29 Like many nuts
32 Northern Spy, for one
34 Concerned
39 Bookstore section
40 Calcutta coverup
41 Chilling, so to speak: 2 wds.
42 "___ Go Bragh!" (Irish)
43 Fish of the perch family
44 Lobster and beluga products

Down

1 Ice cream flavor, for short
2 Airport pickup
3 Tel ___, Israel
4 Discern
5 Oklahoma Indian
6 Coins featuring Pope Benedict XVI
7 Blue ___, sea cave of Capri
8 "The ___ Ranger"
9 Shifting dunes in deserts such as the Sahara
10 Delight, to a hipster
16 P, to Pythagoras
18 Bar bill
19 Diamonds, to hoods
20 "The Princess and the ___"
22 Beer belly
23 Broadway, e.g.
24 'A Shropshire ___' (A.E. Housman work)
28 Drum sound: hyph.
29 More nimble
30 Amber, e.g.
31 Inferior
33 In itself: 2 wds.
34 Greek letter, or a tiny bit
35 Poetic contraction
36 Hawaiian tuber
37 Pennsylvania city on Presque Isle Bay
38 Rackets
39 Cushion

19

Across

1 Invitation request, initially
5 Aquarium owner's bane
10 Safe, on board
11 ___ Field, Mary Todd Lincoln in the 2012 movie "Lincoln"
12 Extensive: hyph.
14 Hook shape
15 Lentil, e.g.
16 Gets on film
18 "___ on Down the Road" ("The Wiz")
22 More, to a minimalist
24 Arrow partner
25 Barter
28 Decrease
30 Costa del ___
31 Baby's first word, maybe
33 Equal
35 Body
39 Beethoven work
41 Balloon filler
42 Labor saver
45 Big-eyed bee
46 Albatross, figuratively
47 Circe, for one
48 "Same time ___ week"

Down

1 Rapid series of short loud sounds
2 Cut drastically, as prices
3 Even-numbered page
4 Hard throw, in baseball
5 Appraise
6 Negligee material
7 Clearing
8 Every little bit
9 Reversible body part, as it were
13 Favor
17 "___ Black Magic"
19 Camel-hair coat
20 Barfly
21 Dolly, for one
23 Indian turnover
25 1/6 fl. oz.
26 Anonymous Wade opponent
27 Microbrew, frequently
29 Block passage through
32 Insight
34 Chopper blade
36 "Common Sense" pamphleteer
37 Crazy Horse, e.g.
38 "Lunar Asparagus" sculptor Max
40 Corn ___
42 Magazine pages, often
43 Altdorf is its capital
44 Heavyweight boxer "Two ___" Tony Galento

20

Across

1. Bite-the-bullet type
6. Biting
11. ___ cotta
12. "Dream ___" (1959 Bobby Darin hit)
13. American dogwood: red ___
14. Cover, in a way
15. All-purpose truck, for short
16. Bass, for one
18. Animal that says "moo"
19. Discussion
21. "What's the ___?"
22. Fond du ___, Wis.
23. Act
24. Norway and Germany, for example
27. Bring tranquility to
28. Ring bearer, maybe
29. "... hmm"
30. From England, Wales, or Scotland, e.g.
34. Alter, in a way
35. Bob Newhart, as Dick Loudon, ran one
36. ___-eyed
37. Mom's relative
39. Spherical objects
41. Less emotional
42. Double-S curves
43. Gives advice
44. Not better

Down

1. Basin for holy water
2. Head, in Italy
3. Architectural projection
4. Bad thing to raise
5. Parade
6. Birch relative
7. ___ anglais (English horn)
8. One leaving before a storm
9. Uses a couch, maybe
10. Like tea
17. Stand
20. Booster, perhaps
23. Embarrassing info, to the tabloids
24. Fall in pitch of the voice
25. Elderly spinster: 2 wds.
26. Colorful arc seen after a storm
27. Estate sharer
30. Coffin holders
31. Do-nothing
32. They're underfoot
33. "Demian" author
38. Tiger's start, in two different ways
40. "Give it ___!"

21

Across

1 Mine roof prop
6 Starchy foodstuff used in making puddings
10 Beauty queens' crowns
12 Flamboyance
13 With hands on hips
14 Theater section
15 Craving
16 But
18 Random wreckage
21 Au courant
23 Towards the back, on a ship
26 Creature fought by Harry Potter
27 Cries of sorrow and grief
29 Navigator's need
30 Rider's foot support
32 Syndicate
33 Italian sausage
36 Mischievous one
39 Birthright-for-pottage trader
40 ___ Babies (popular dolls)
43 Conclusion starter
44 First-born
45 Jekyll's alter ego
46 Customs

Down

1 Dog command
2 ___'s Peak, one of Colorado's 53 fourteeners
3 It can fall from the sky
4 Coat part
5 Go on and on
6 Exchanges for money
7 Cream additive
8 Comedian's stock
9 Singles
11 Becomes unpleasant
17 Birdbrain
19 Moray, e.g.
20 Certain fir
21 Cash dispenser, initially
22 Car grille protector
23 Frequent flier
24 Bird ___
25 80 minims: abbr.
28 "___ you joking?"
31 Cheyenne, Chippewa or Cherokee
32 Reason
33 Actor Green of the "Austin Powers" series
34 Far from ruddy
35 Extol
37 ___-en-scène
38 Animals at home
41 "Slippery" tree
42 Shakespeare's "Much ___ About Nothing"

22

Across

1   Attell and Goldstein
5   Record label founded in 1974
11 Characterization
12 Meteorological phenomenon in the Pacific: 2 wds.
13 Teatro ___ Scala, Milan venue
14 Slender and elegant
15 Welfare eligibility assessments: 2 wds.
17 Loses heat
18 Enter cautiously: 2 wds.
21 Falco of "Nurse Jackie"
25 Battery type, initially
26 Noah's boat
27 Attention-getters
29 John of "Fawlty Towers"
32 Shoe-factory employee
34 Chinese snack: 2 wds.
39 Font flourishes
40 Wings of an insect
41 It hangs around in the winter
42 Diplomatic quality
43 Thyroid enlargement
44 Chevy model

Down

1   "My Name Is ___" (William Saroyan story collection)
2   Tree trunk
3   Jazz great Fitzgerald
4   Meeting with a medium
5   R&B singer Gerald of The Manhattans
6   French composer Maurice
7   Existing: 2 wds.
8   Bank deposit?
9   Blows up, initially
10 Org. for dentists
16 "___ Married an Axe Murderer" (Mike Myers film): 2 wds.
18 "The Raven" author's monogram
19 "___ in alpha": 2 wds.
20 Gained a lap
22 Daniel ___ Kim, founder of 3AD
23 Apr. addressee
24 Make (out)
28 Inflexible about rules
29 Church burner
30 Chair part
31 Typos
33 Winchester, e.g.
34 Dry, like Spanish wine
35 Toyota hybrids
36 Patron saint of Norway
37 Shoe string
38 Mother of Artemis
39 Type of newsgroup, initially

23

Across

1. Cornrow's place
6. Proto or ecto suffix
11. Dearest
12. From now onward
13. Performer
15. Bar stock
16. Big part of a hare
17. Black cuckoo
18. Anderson and Bowersox
20. Medicinal pill
22. Coil of thread
23. Peruvian money
24. Assassinated
26. Brought on board
30. Knock off
32. All's alternative
33. Carved figure
36. Mouthful
37. Close one
38. Double-crosser
40. "Yes, ___!"
41. Resourceful, enterprising
44. Era
45. Hair for lions
46. A deadly sin
47. "Keep Out" and "Danger"

Down

1. Arab chiefs: var.
2. Hide
3. Bug part
4. Bruce of martial arts
5. Combustible heap
6. Ruler in ancient Egypt
7. It's made of flowers in Hawaii
8. One year's record
9. Embarrassing public fight
10. ___ badge (boy scout's award)
14. Makes lace
19. Tutu, for one
21. Flashy jewelry, slangily
25. Feed
27. Stirring up
28. Animate
29. Bring down
31. Seed in a pod
33. Meat skewers
34. Dravidian language
35. "Remember the ___!"
39. Highland toppers
42. Come into possession of
43. ___ chi (martial art)

24

Across

1 Wife of Esau
5 Small blister on the skin
9 Andean capital
10 1887 Verdi opera
13 Dentist: 2 wds.
15 "Catch-22" author Joseph
16 Take to the seas
17 "___ recall ...": 2 wds.
18 Hoops grp.
20 La lead-in
21 Put one's foot down
23 "Cock-a-Doodle Dandy" playwright Seán
25 "Up" star Ed
27 Gladiatorial sites
30 Cotton bundle
34 Filling station filler
35 Incidentally, initially
37 Tarnish
38 Follower of John
40 Eminence
42 Have similar views: 4 wds.
44 Trailer, in modern lingo
45 Vigoda and Saperstein
46 Dissolve
47 "B.C." cartoonist Johnny

Down

1 Hawaiian welcomes
2 Most desperate
3 Charlotte ___, Virgin Islands
4 Lecture room
5 New Orleans hot spot: 2 wds.
6 USPS delivery, e.g.
7 Brain activity records, initially
8 Sheep's cries
11 River of Orléans
12 Replacement for a tooth cusp
14 D.C. figure
19 Expert in strikes
22 Slam
24 Short trader?
26 Day of rest and worship: abbr.
27 Slack-jawed
28 Speed demon
29 High regard
31 Microscopic creature
32 Attorney
33 "Airwolf" actor Borgnine
36 Moisten with water
39 Golfer Ballesteros
41 Genesis shipwright
43 Brynner of "The King and I"

25

Across

1 Biblical son of Shem
5 European "boot"
10 Equivalent
11 Jackie's predecessor
12 Operation for a new heart, e.g.
14 Literary contraction
15 Has in one's hands
16 18th and 19th century artists Rembrandt, Raphael, Rubens and Titian
18 Brit. dictionaries
21 Wide widths, initially
23 River to the English Channel
24 Cherubs
27 Cantor or Murphy
29 Seafood restaurant sign "Oysters ___ season": 2 wds.
30 Spy Mata ___
32 Run ___ in the paper: 2 wds.
34 Occupies, as a table: 2 wds.
38 French cup
40 Highest note in Guido's scale
41 It's hit by a racket: 2 wds.
43 Turner and Wood
44 The Bee Gees, e.g.
45 Tomb
46 Applications

Down

1 "___ Too Far" ("Aida" song): 2 wds.
2 Spectacle on the sidewalk
3 Big appliance maker
4 Fraternity members
5 Inconvenience
6 Lofty
7 Argentine V.P. Boudou
8 Oil source
9 Eventually
13 Exclamation of exasperation
17 Celtic Neptune
19 511, to Nero
20 Perceive
22 Set
24 The Altar constellation
25 Not max.
26 Running wild: 3 wds.
28 Morse code click
31 Help
33 Jack's son in "The Shining"
35 Cooks over high heat
36 "Kate & ___"
37 Giant, bronze automaton given to Europa by Zeus
39 Cinch
41 Warm bedside manner, initially
42 Heat unit, for short

Across

1 Place of worship
7 French key
10 James Bond movie of 2008, "Quantum of ___"
11 Coughed up
12 Code word for "S"
13 "The Andy Griffith Show" lad
14 Coward
16 Prone to acne, say
19 "My Big Fat Greek Wedding" star Vardalos
20 Inched
22 Mixer with O.J., popularly
26 Chaos
27 Biology lab stain
28 Make petty comments
29 Construction girder: hyph.
30 Polite shorthand abbr.
32 Name in "Nine Stories"
33 NBC news program
37 Exploitative type
38 Marked with spots
42 Chest muscles, briefly
43 Ford of fashion
44 Biblical verb ending
45 Rest periods

Down

1 Authors Lewis and Forester, initially
2 ___ polloi
3 Cream ___
4 They go off with a bang at celebrations: hyph.
5 Brown shade
6 Come to know
7 Spanish cloak
8 53, to a Roman
9 Willa Cather co-biographer Leon
11 Destructive black-and-yellow insect: 2 wds.
15 Japanese-American group
16 "I Ain't Marching Anymore" singer
17 Persia, now
18 ___ Strauss & Co.
21 Immune response orchestrator: hyph.
23 Suffix for abnormalities
24 First name of the star of "Schindler's List"
25 "You've Got a Friend ___" ("Toy Story" tune): 2 wds.
31 Flip of a hit single: 2 wds.
33 Copy, briefly
34 At ___ time (prearranged): 2 wds.
35 Kind of support, shortly
36 Pinot ___ (dry red wine)
39 High ___
40 Cry of mock horror
41 Internet protocol, initially

27

Across

1 Expression of displeasure

6 Break up the lumps

10 Calm down

11 Quito's country: abbr.

12 F.B.I. sting of the 1970–80s

13 Sketch

14 ___ Offensive

15 Muscle quality

17 Pitt of "Burn After Reading"

19 Japanese automaker

23 International real estate company

25 ___ Dhabi

26 Nilsson and Sills, e.g.: 2 wds.

29 South African political party, initially

30 Overseas assembly

31 Plays for theater

33 Pant

36 "Norma Rae" director

38 Iowa college

39 Ingrid's role in "Casablanca"

42 Mountain mentioned in Genesis

44 High school student, usually

45 Acrobatic springs: hyph.

46 Start for a plant

47 Lollapalooza

Down

1 Judicious

2 Country, capital San José: 2 wds.

3 Stock page letters

4 Question start

5 Kid's way to make money: 2 wds.

6 Tennis champ Monica

7 In this localité

8 "Fee, Fi, Fo, ___"

9 Beachgoer's acquisition

10 Letters identifying the four voices in a choir

16 37th president of the USA

18 Like L.B.J.

20 Town in western California on Monterey Bay: 2 wds.

21 Legal org.

22 Fraternity letters

24 Kenyan tribesman

26 Hippie's home

27 Time off, initially

28 Henpeck

32 "___ Mrs. Smith" (2005): 2 wds.

34 Covered with suds

35 Darlings

37 Crosby, Stills and Nash, e.g.

39 "___ just what I've always wanted!"

40 Wranglers alternative

41 Get the picture

43 G.I.'s mail drop

28

Across

1 They guard sacks
8 Deface
11 Gate-crash
12 Buzz
13 Place for civil cases: 2 wds.
15 Hosts
16 "Here ___, there..." (kids' song lyric): 2 wds.
17 Brief shots?
18 Light ___ (insubstantial): 2 wds.
19 ___ Paulo (Brazilian city)
20 Expresses disapproval: hyph.
22 Pop-up breakfast fare
23 Anointing as part of a religious ceremony
26 Cut off
29 ___ bourguignon
30 Sagan of "Cosmos"
31 Sheryl Crow's "___ Wanna Do": 2 wds.
32 Extent-wise: 2 wds.
34 In silence
36 Ramat ___ (Israeli city)
37 District under the care of a bishop
38 Cyprinoid fish
39 Carpenter, at times

Down

1 They have pull
2 Inability to recall the names of everyday objects
3 Masonry finish applied when wet
4 Pelagic soarers
5 Quiet
6 "Grand" ice cream maker
7 IBM competitor
8 Terrorize or threaten: hyph.
9 Canny
10 Electric motor parts
14 Drying houses
18 Heaps and heaps: 2 wds.
20 Cry of relief, initially
21 Actor Tognazzi
22 iPod cases, in France
23 African river
24 Commission-free: hyph.
25 Singer Dion
26 Don who pitched the only perfect World Series game
27 "You won't like the alternative": 2 wds.
28 Cast member
30 Maine's ___ Bay
32 Nastase of the courts
33 Dodge model
35 Aug. hours in Akron

29

Across

1 Petty quarrels
6 Smeltery refuse
10 Addition symbol
11 Rising star
13 Fifth-century inhabitants of England: hyph.
15 Actress Myrna
16 PIN requester
17 Speed (up), in short
18 Afghan monetary unit
19 Draft dispenser
20 Dadaist Hans
21 Cut off
23 Electrical pioneer Nikola
25 Listening
27 Peaks
29 Chinese dollar
33 Telekinesis, e.g.
34 Be abed
36 Fundraising org.
37 Dated
38 Govt. health watchdog
39 Knows, old-style
40 Embroidery resembling tapestry
43 Ghostlike
44 Afterwards
45 "Hey there!"
46 Church officer

Down

1 Resells (tickets) for a big profit
2 Come to fruition: 2 wds.
3 Paisley alternative
4 ___ Aviv, Israel
5 Summer ermine
6 Run with quick light steps
7 Fish for breakfast
8 Of easy virtue
9 Family subdivisions
12 Common request, initially
14 In the continental U.S.
22 Mother: var.
24 Hog's heaven
26 Handout on the street
27 Nodding
28 Apple products
30 Against the direction of the breeze
31 Immediately: 2 wds.
32 Talk casually
33 Southern dish
35 Expire, as a subscription
41 Bad-mouth, slangily
42 Crude stuff

30

Across

1. Stars and Stripes, e.g.
5. "Aladdin" prince and namesakes
9. City in Parker County, Texas
10. Cattle farm
12. "Such a pity": 2 wds.
13. "___ you!" (challenging phrase): 2 wds.
14. Wall St. wheeler-dealer
15. Harvest goddess
17. Depressed
18. Modern: prefix
19. Diaper wearer
20. Pier gp.
21. Part of N.A.A.C.P.: abbr.
23. Becomes tangled
25. Credited to noted artist Romain de Tirtoff
27. Mint, e.g.
30. One of Chekhov's "Three Sisters"
34. Neighbor of Iran: abbr.
35. Like some answers
37. One billion years
38. "What Kind of Fool ___?": 2 wds.
39. Whiskey-mash ingredient
40. Big wine holder
41. Shopper's binge
43. Big hotel room
45. Swings around
46. Rate of travel
47. Items included in envs.
48. Campaign staffer

Down

1. Largest of the Lesser Sunda Islands, Indonesia
2. Greek island in the eastern Aegean Sea
3. Toothpaste recommenders, initially
4. "Waiting for ___" Samuel Beckett play
5. Botanical beards
6. Scot's son
7. Caught ___ (being dishonest): 3 wds.
8. Ancient rolled document
9. Posture adopted in hatha yoga
11. "___ Beautiful" (Cleo Laine song): 2 wds.
16. Depict
22. Not old, in Berlin
24. Poverty-fighting grp.
26. Bottle up (feelings, for example)
27. Bridge declaration: 2 wds.
28. Try
29. Snow-covered slope: 2 wds.
31. Imposed (a tax)
32. Narrow chin-tuft
33. Put in a stake
36. Actress Thompson of "Dear White People"
42. Common Market letters, once
44. News letters

31

Across

1 Passbook abbr.
4 WWW pop-ups, e.g.
7 Snow, in Scotland
10 France's Belle-____
11 Cubs play here
12 Half a score
13 Hillshire Brands company: 2 wds.
15 Average: abbr.
16 Go (through), as evidence
17 Break away
19 Foe
21 Heaven's opposite
22 Calendar abbr.
23 Fairy tale figures
26 Maria ____, (1717–80) Archduchess of Austria
28 Criticize maliciously
30 End-of-the-century year
33 Carpenter's wedge
34 Field Marshal of World War II, ____ von Bock
36 Diners
39 Mötley ____ (Nikki Sixx's band)
40 Mil. decoration
41 Part of London that includes the Docklands: 2 wds.
43 Extreme
44 Constellation near Scorpius
45 Pou ____, standing place
46 Carried out
47 "Greetings" org.

Down

1 Put down, slangily
2 "Ishtar" director May
3 Ability to reproduce a musical note accurately: 2 wds.
4 Jewish org. founded in 1913
5 Bad marks
6 Bygone blade
7 Application info: 2 wds.
8 Sewing item
9 Heavenly messengers
14 Cash cache initials
18 Xs to the Greeks
20 River of Belgium
24 Couples, briefly
25 Atoll protector
27 Blood pigment
28 Geopolitical org. that includes The Philippines and Brunei
29 Part of a column between the base and the capital
31 Recites numbers in ascending order
32 Statements of belief
35 Outside: prefix
37 Go through volumes
38 Draped dress
42 Feeling low

32

Across

1 "Norma Rae" director
5 Eye, at the Eiffel Tower
9 Agitated
11 Funny Youngman
12 College in Atherton, California
13 Mix with, as seasonings: 2 wds.
14 Greet at the door: 2 wds.
16 Suffix with Capri
17 ___ tai (drink)
19 "And the whole earth ___ one language" (Genesis 11:1): 2 wds.
21 Start of a Shakespeare title
23 Not invincible
26 Foot-long stick, often
28 Taj ___
29 Hide: 2 wds.
31 Element removed from gasoline
32 Joint appraiser
34 More: Sp.
35 Denver clock setting, initially
37 First part of a song, shortly
39 Brown ermine
41 First word of a counting rhyme
44 Kind of ray
45 Under, in Umbria
46 "___ Little Tenderness": 2 wds.
47 Item of footwear

Down

1 Mate for a ewe
2 "May ___ excused?": 2 wds.
3 Certain throat operation
4 Install terrazzo, e.g.
5 Brit. lexicon
6 Pressure time for many salespeople: 4 wds.
7 "What's ___ for me?": 2 wds.
8 "Fatal Attraction" director Adrian
10 Movie mogul Marcus
11 Two-wheeled cab for two
15 "___ the eggman..." (Beatles line): 2 wds.
17 Clay-sand mixture
18 To him in France: 2 wds.
20 Buccal
22 Ward of "Once and Again"
24 Laser-pointer battery, initially
25 Attys.' degrees
27 Ghost town in Custer County, Colorado
30 Skin blemish
33 Mail carriers have them: abbr.
35 N.C.O. rank
36 ___ chamber
38 Early models had eight-horsepower engines, initially
40 Dr.'s org.
42 "What Am ___ You?" (2004 Norah Jones single): 2 wds.
43 Nondiscriminating hirer in help wanted ads, initially

33

Across

1 Make dirty
7 Create dresses
10 Edge, trounce: 2 wds.
11 Granite State sch.
12 Not essential
14 Author of "Heart of Darkness" Joseph
15 Supercomputer inventor Seymour
16 ___ Kringle (Santa Claus)
17 Feudal lord
18 John Coltrane instrument, briefly
19 Takes a nap
21 ___ motion (start): 2 wds.
22 Angels of the highest order
25 Dance bit
28 Some 1980s Chryslers: 2 wds.
29 Indefinite amount
30 Biblical prophet
31 More sensitive, as hearing
33 Adolescent pop music fan
35 Ruler divs.
36 Atlantic island
37 It's tipped by an admirer
38 Puts down

Down

1 Mrs., in Mexico
2 1960s–70s TV sleuth
3 Anatomical canals
4 Brown & Haley candy, Almond ___
5 Gave prompts to
6 City map abbr.
7 Ray of PBS's "NewsHour"
8 Make one's blood boil
9 "Indeed!": 2 wds.
10 Dollars, slangily
13 Boxy Toyota product
17 ___ Lane (Clark Kent's co-worker)
19 Fall mos.
20 Kind of power
21 It's a wrap
22 Drawing
23 Itchy rash
24 Hardest to locate
25 Entree with a crust: 2 wds.
26 Foreign heads of state: var.
27 Spanish missionary Junipero
29 Building managers, slangily
31 Basic verse option
32 Musical conclusion
34 Singer Sumac

34

Across

1 Sum up, for short
6 Wheat grown as stock feed
11 Love, in Lourdes
12 Beauty pageant wear
13 Low-grade wool
14 Attachment: hyph.
15 Brewski, slangily
17 Perform John Cage's "4'33"," e.g.
18 ___ War
20 Alter a "Life" sentence?
22 Be human, perhaps
23 Journal
26 Al Green, e.g.
27 ___ Today
28 "Gee whiz!"
29 "___: make my day!": 2 wds.
31 Barely get by (with "out")
32 Relate, as a story
33 Brit. tax system, initially
34 Gas leak evidence
36 "___ is the last straw!"
38 Wet, weatherwise
40 Deck out
43 Papal court
44 Commotion
45 Crosswise, on deck
46 Barely visible to the naked eye

Down

1 Ewe's mate
2 "Down under" fowl
3 College of arts
4 Foreshadow
5 Egg on
6 Pilot's announcement, briefly
7 Central vein of a leaf
8 Bespoke: 3 wds.
9 "Aeneid" figure
10 Let off steam, maybe
16 Condiment from the deep: 2 wds.
18 "Lulu" composer
19 Cookie with a "Double Stuf" variety
21 Tennis doubles team, e.g.
23 Face-off
24 Like some Chardonnay
25 "Trick" joint
30 Rupture
33 Arouse, as anger
34 "Free Willy" creature
35 Smear, like paint
37 Bulk
39 It's like a sweet potato
41 Physicist's study
42 ___ into (be nosy about)

35

Across

1 "___ a Dance" (John Michael Montgomery album of 1992)
6 Grain husks
11 Coastal feature
12 "Daphnis et ___"
13 Funny Anne
14 Photo tint
15 Aching
17 Quite: 2 wds.
18 Fin or Finn follower
20 Cry loudly
22 W.W. I army, initially
23 "___ seems": 2 wds.
25 Grand story
27 "Olympia" painter
29 Dow cousin: 3 wds.
32 Shipping allowance
34 Comic-strip light bulb
35 Syllable of dismissal
37 Songstress Starr
39 Common deciduous tree
40 Robert who played A.J. Soprano
42 "Yes, ___"
44 Bite on, as a puppy: 2 wds.
46 Escalator feature
49 Firefighter Red
50 Two under par, on a hole
51 Carl's friend in "The Simpsons"
52 Employees

Down

1 Boundary, briefly
2 Suffix with elephant
3 Short-lived success: 4 wds.
4 Architect Saarinen (1910–61)
5 Hollywood Walk of Fame sights
6 N.C.A.A. football ranking system
7 Stat start
8 The beginning and the end, in the Bible: 3 wds.
9 Hubbub
10 ___ Marmara: 2 wds.
16 Goddess of the dawn
18 Ending for classic or colonial
19 Insurance assessors' org.: inits.
21 Degs. for historians and linguists
24 Prefix with centenary
26 Toujours ___
28 Boston Red Sox captain's nickname
30 Raiding grp.
31 Islamabad's country: abbr.
33 One may be worn with a kilt
35 Important exam
36 Say "y'all," say
38 Eastwood in Rawhide
41 Drops from the sky
43 Lillian Jackson Braun's "The Cat Who Smelled ___": 2 wds.
45 Give it a whirl
47 1936 candidate Landon
48 Absolutely brilliant, in slang

36

Across

1 Can convenience: hyph.

7 Bernadette, e.g.: abbr.

10 Kind of pudding

11 "Huh?" sounds

12 Cold War symbol: 2 wds.

14 Green in Grenoble

15 "___ Ben Johnson" (inscription on a tomb): 2 wds.

16 "I'm ___ you!" ("You don't fool me!")

17 Banded metamorphic rock

18 Pou ___, basis of operation

19 Bach's "___ of Fugue": 2 wds.

20 Unfriendliness

21 Princess Fiona in "Shrek," e.g.

23 "Gunsmoke" bartender

26 French analytical chemist (1754–1826)

27 "You're Laughing ___" (Irving Berlin song): 2 wds.

28 Bit of clowning

29 A long way from wealthy

30 Redundant records: 2 wds.

33 Wore away

34 Against the law

35 Key grip workplace

36 Library desk

Down

1 Mother or father

2 City north of Lisbon, Portugal

3 Ford model named for a horse

4 It has a lot of chapters, initially

5 Prefix with pressure

6 Maria von Trapp's title

7 Beach atmosphere: 2 wds.

8 Physiological need to drink

9 Old laborers

10 Certain television recorders

13 Pick up the tab

17 Hamlet's father, e.g.

19 "Ooh la la!": 2 wds.

20 Apple, e.g.

21 Victorian, in a way

22 Prepared to race: 2 wds.

23 Any of a comedic trio

24 Ethically indifferent

25 Streep of "It's Complicated"

26 Dads

27 Better suited

31 Labor group, initially

32 Certain camera, for short

37

Across

1. Rebels
8. ABC morning show, for short
11. Oath
12. "You dirty ___!"
13. Mole: 2 wds.
15. Holdings
16. Decorative case
17. Angry, with "off"
18. Shaquille of the N.B.A.
19. Group of schools in one area, for short
20. Ape's cousin
22. Infant's illness
23. Anon
26. Dracula, at times
29. Actor Quinn
30. Gem that can be carved
31. Dudley Do-Right's org.
32. ___ dictum
34. Tony Danza sitcom
36. Department of eastern France
37. Accord
38. Marked a ballot, maybe
39. "Guys and Dolls" composer/lyricist Frank

Down

1. Additional data on a news story
2. Non-poetic writing forms
3. Stirred up
4. Fix firmly: var.
5. Bank deposit?
6. Mexican men, colloquially
7. "Twenty Thousand Leagues Under the ___"
8. Humperdinck heroine
9. Owner's guidebook
10. Emperor who died on his wedding night
14. Photo finish?
18. At first: abbr.
20. Thug
21. Former name of the cable network Versus, initially
22. Applauds
23. Swab target
24. Fonzie's red-haired pal
25. Dumas's Dantès
26. Marching band sticks
27. "___ Fideles"
28. Less verbose
30. Agrees
32. "Yikes!": 2 wds.
33. Jean Renoir film "La ___ Humaine"
35. Address book no.

38

Across

1 Oscilloscope part, initially
4 Male sheep, in Britain
7 Conned
10 Catalyst for Pinocchio
11 Retrovirus component, initially
12 "___ moment, please"
13 100 percent
14 Pop-ups, usually
15 Blaster, initially
16 Small smoked sausages
18 "I told you so!" laugh
19 Category
20 Blunder
21 Spenders' binges
23 Blood letters
24 Fla. neighbor
25 Fraternity letter
27 Mafia boss
28 Afternoon break, perhaps
29 Fuse unit
31 Degree in math?
32 Hair holder
33 "That's painful!"
34 Kind of gland
37 Cuckoo bird
38 "Flying Down to ___"
39 Big time
40 Elton John, e.g.
41 Dash widths
42 Break a Commandment
43 Cubes in the freezer
44 Conceit
45 Down in the dumps

Down

1 Dog's scratcher
2 Anger
3 Message carrier once: 2 wds.
4 Apprentice
5 Comprehension
6 Antiquated
7 Impetuosity
8 Michegan city: 2 wds.
9 Oust
17 French word before a maiden name
21 Hindu religious mendicant
22 Passionless
26 Type of sweetened sherry
30 Author Edgar Allan ___
32 Ranee's wrap: var.
35 Diva's song
36 About 30% of the earth's surface

39

Across

1. "___ Freischütz" (Weber opera)
4. Dublin dance
7. Affairs
10. The ___ Glove ("As Seen on TV" mitt)
11. "I'll take that as ___": 2 wds.
12. It's found in banks
13. Open tract
14. Hwy. that begins in Astoria, NY
15. Suffix with effect
16. Difficult, laborious
18. College football ranking format: inits.
19. Abundantly
21. Mozart's No. 1 through No. 41, briefly
22. Cotton fabric with a shiny finish
23. Clad
25. Expire: 2 wds.
27. Ashcroft's predecessor
30. Final results of a manufacturing process: 2 wds.
32. Cut, as trees
33. Butcher's offering
34. Enzyme suffix
35. "Whom have ___ heaven but you?" Psalms 73:25: 2 wds.
36. Immigrant's class, briefly
37. Letters used (by some) for dates
38. Peck at
39. I-95, e.g.: abbr.
40. Pacifier
41. "Do Ya" rock grp.
42. Initials on old Asian maps

Down

1. Exercise in lanes: 2 wds.
2. Either singer of "Cathy's Clown"
3. Poker-table phrase: 4 wds.
4. Frilly neckpiece
5. Offensively prying
6. Travels a long way: 2 wds.
7. Some railroad cars: hyph.
8. Cassandra, e.g.
9. Generator element
17. Clear
20. Womb
24. Wind farm sight
25. Clinics, in short
26. Agency the U.S. rejoined in 2003
28. Los Alamos experiments, in headlines: 2 wds.
29. Stable worker
31. "Meat in the Middle!" dog treat brand

40

Across

1 Portuguese territory
6 The Underworld, to Ancient Greeks
11 Lab gels
12 Scrub, NASA-style
13 Having a key center
14 Finnish steam room
15 Manhattan Project goal: hyph.
17 Plead for a treat, dog-style
18 Hospital fixtures
20 Ring, as bells
22 Self-proclaimed psychic Geller
23 Eternal
26 Iranian money
28 Cheesy snack
29 Bible book
31 Hold up
32 Defeated
33 Spinning toys
34 Eggs
36 Second-year students, for short
38 Type measurements
40 Artist's support
43 Bread spread
44 "___ Mine" (1985 sci-fi movie)
45 Cool, lustrous fabric
46 As such: 2 wds.

Down

1 Pin cushion?
2 From long ___
3 Breakfast buffet choice: 2 wds.
4 Ishmael's people
5 1952 Olympics host
6 Ex-stars: hyph.
7 J.D.'s org.
8 Two-timer: hyph.
9 Coastal raptor
10 Like bachelor parties
16 Gas-guzzling stat.
18 Town, informally
19 Lake that feeds Niagara Falls
21 French menu phrase: 2 wds.
23 Hired killer
24 Boutique
25 Breaks down, in a way
27 "I Hope You Dance" singer ___ Ann Womack
30 City in Japan
33 Macbeth, for one
34 Fiery gemstone
35 King Henry ___
37 Birdcall
39 Ginger ___ (soft drink)
41 Bad ___, German spa
42 Caustic chemical

41

Across

1 Barbecue fuel
6 Ladies of the house, informally
11 "___ Road" (Beatles album)
12 Call off, at Cape Canaveral
13 Daniel Boone, notably
15 Little bird
16 Big belly
17 Certain tropical cuckoo
18 "Do the Right Thing" director Spike
19 Dig up dandelions, maybe
20 Churchill's "so few," initially
21 Bounds
23 African fly
25 "Oklahoma!" aunt
27 Edible legume
30 Cut
34 Gasteyer of "Mean Girls"
35 Do film work
37 Monetary unit of Romania
38 Cook Co.'s home
39 Drops in the morning meadow
40 Container's top
41 Tiny time period
44 OH- or Cl-, chemically
45 Part of a spur
46 Cardinal flats
47 Band on the run?

Down

1 Kine
2 "Access Hollywood" cohost
3 Died down
4 "Fantasy Island" prop
5 Slender woman
6 Lap dog
7 Legal letters
8 "Amadeus" composer
9 Rupp, Arco, et al.
10 Friction
14 Footwear securers
22 Back-to-school mo.
24 .0000001 joule
26 Warm-up acts: hyph.
27 Alligator's cousin
28 Surfing, perhaps
29 "Casablanca" producer
31 Concedes
32 Fishing nets
33 Powwow
36 Dweeb
42 Auction offering
43 Pigeon English?

42

Across

1 Church service
5 Figures of speech
11 ___ du jour (dish of the day)
12 Hardly, if ever
13 Angel's headwear
14 Call for
15 Common chord
17 One with a beat
18 Creatures from outer space
20 Fractional ending
21 Give a bad review to
22 Instinctive
24 Artist's asset
25 Bobby of Boston Bruins fame
26 86,400 seconds
29 Oolong, for one
30 Choler
31 Curative waters locale
34 Computer devices: hyph.
36 Spring Break souvenir, maybe
37 Absolute
38 Mom's sister
40 Drone, e.g.
43 Milk and water, e.g.
44 Mosque V.I.P.
45 Boneless piece of fish
46 Forbidden: var.

Down

1 Dashboard inits.
2 Montgomery is its cap.
3 Soup cracker
4 Target, for one
5 Pirate hoard: 2 wds.
6 "We the Living" author Ayn
7 Food scrap
8 Christmas wish, for many
9 "Four Quartets" poet
10 Imaginary spirit of the air
16 Bullion unit
18 Gibbon, for one
19 Ballad
23 Business
26 Miniature 3D scene with figures
27 Chair part
28 "Without a doubt!"
31 Employees
32 St. ___ Girl, Beck's Brewery offering
33 Make void, as a marriage
35 Send, as payment
37 Fries, often
39 "Shop ___ you drop"
41 DNA testing facility
42 Ostrich look-alike

43

Across

1 Blood component

7 ___ talk

10 Wealth

11 Pivot

12 Sung dramas

13 Container weight

14 Lift

16 Senior person

18 African animal

19 Egghead

23 He shrugged, in an Ayn Rand title

26 Gumdrop flavor

27 Uncertainties

29 Choose (with "for")

30 Due to

33 Alert

36 Western blue flag, e.g.

37 Cooking directions

41 Camera piece

42 Bewitch

43 Account

44 Parti-colored

Down

1 In favor of

2 Griffin Dunne comedy, "___ Service"

3 Serve right on the T, often

4 Bit

5 Breakfast, lunch and dinner

6 Pluses

7 ___ du jour

8 100 cents, sometimes

9 ___-reviewed journals

11 Keep food from

15 Butcher's offering

16 "I'm ___ you!" ("You don't fool me!")

17 "Little" comic strip character

18 "Crikey!"

20 "Famous" cookie guy

21 "Forget it!"

22 Letters that are Wile E. Coyote's undoing, often

24 "The Sound of Music" figure

25 Hasenpfeffer, e.g.

28 Chicken

31 Hippodrome, e.g.

32 Open, as a bottle

33 "___ 'er up!"

34 Sundae topper, perhaps

35 Ali's milieu

38 Dennis the Menace, e.g.

39 Running expert, for short

40 "…I'll be there ___ long" (Cohan lyric)

44

Across

1 Mischief maker
4 Grazing locale
7 Call to Bo-peep
8 Van Gogh cut off his ___
9 Est. as to when the trip ends
12 On purpose
15 Challenges
16 Geometry calculation
17 Carbon compound
18 Low comment
19 Fortify
20 Nonreligious type
23 Small pouches for shampoo, etc.
25 Dash a liquid against
27 Day divs.
30 Advertising award
31 Synagogue
32 Reddish salon dye
34 Relaxed
35 Stream, e.g.
37 Equine critter
38 Scoundrel
39 Frostiness
40 "If only ___ listened …"
41 Approximately

Down

1 In the same place: Lat.
2 Tomorrow, in Toledo
3 Denis to France, and Patrick to Ireland, e.g.: 2 wds.
4 Cataract site
5 ___ one's words (recant)
6 Part of a score, maybe
9 Alto woodwind instruments
10 Anklebone
11 On guard
13 Elusive one
14 Beginning
20 Masquerade
21 Everyday article
22 That gal
24 Do penance
25 Pronunciation symbol
26 Declarations of innocence
28 Muscovite, for one
29 One of the Seven Dwarfs
31 Measly tip
33 Crafty
34 Prayer start
36 Pool stick

45

Across

1. The "A" in James A. Garfield
6. Weapon often seen on "24"
11. Money, in slang
12. Chicago airport
13. Less well
14. Swindler, slangily
15. Alternative to shaving cream
16. Battery type, initially
18. J. Edgar Hoover once ran it
19. Bonanza find
20. Letterman's network letters
21. Bleed
22. Killer whales
24. Peace of mInd
25. Man-made reservoir
27. Boys in the 'hood
29. "Smart" ones
31. Gamboling spot
32. Seven, on a sundial
33. "___ be an honor!"
35. Photo-___ (politician's engagements, shortly)
36. "One by one" marcher of song
37. Catch a glimpse of
38. Birth-related
40. Concerning an Andean empire
42. Muralist Rivera
43. Christmas ___
44. Mistake
45. Past, present or future

Down

1. Friend, in Mexico
2. "10" music
3. Amusement park ride: 2 wds.
4. Beer
5. Rattles
6. "Animal House" party costumes
7. "Brilliant!"
8. Certain Californian native: 2 wds.
9. Antarctic volcanic peak
10. Process sugar
17. Forbear
23. U.S.S.R. successor
24. Browning's "before"
26. Snob
27. Flaxen-haired
28. Fix
30. Incredible bargains
32. Guts
34. Heavy, like a muffin
39. In the past
41. Born, in France

49

46

Across

1 Animal track
6 Onetime Golden Arches' offering
11 Cheyenne shelter
12 Gold braid
13 Most important boy- or girlfriend, slangily: 2 wds.
15 Match ender, for short
16 Suffix with chant or mass
17 "___ the winter of our discontent" (Richard III opening line)
19 "China Beach" setting, in short
22 Food eaten on a spring holiday: 2 wds.
24 Internet writing system with unconventional spelling
26 Eight: prefix
27 "Charade" actor: 2 wds.
31 Internet protocol inits.
32 Knitted scarf
33 Prefix with drama
34 Cove
37 Shrill: hyph.
41 Malayan boats
42 Final Commandment
43 Militant movement
44 ___ ghost (hallucinates): 2 wds.

Down

1 Bank acct. report
2 Pinnacle
3 First novel in Cather's "Great Plains" trilogy: 2 wds.
4 Vintner's prefix
5 Mends, as a bad stitching job
6 Puddinglike dessert
7 Algonquian Indian
8 "Still ___" (1999 rap song)
9 ___ Lemon, Tina Fey's "30 Rock" character
10 Lao-___
14 Give up
18 Like some high-fiber cereal
19 Juicy fruit
20 Contract negotiator: abbr.
21 Tropical fruit, briefly
23 Rice-a-___, the San Francisco treat
24 ___ Soundsystem, dance-punk band
25 Suffix with Jacob
28 Rock with colored bands
29 Be a monarch
30 Cancels
33 Assigner of Gs and Rs, initially
35 QB's misfires
36 Turkish leader
37 N.T. book
38 First name in Notre Dame football
39 Data storage site, initially
40 Gnarls Barkley member ___-Lo

47

Across

1 Cookie eaten with ice cream
6 Dentist's directive
11 Long, soft feather
12 More aloof
13 ____ badge (boy scout's award)
14 Three-time French Open winner
15 Hip-hop's rhythmic foundation
17 Bruce Springsteen's "____ the One"
19 Golfing great ____ Trevino
20 Danger to divers
21 Tentacled sea creatures
24 Fish garnish
26 "Enough already!": 2 wds.
28 Try to hit (a mosquito, e.g.): 2 wds.
30 Scale notes
31 Lobbying grp.
32 Teen outbreak
33 City of Honshu
37 Product of the oak tree
38 Ankle bones
41 "You say you ____ revolution…" (Beatles lyric): 2 wds.
42 One sporting three stars: abbr., 2 wds.
43 ____ light: filmmaking arc lamp
44 Late hotelier Helmsley

Down

1 Typing speed measure, initially
2 Drink that comes in a pint
3 Pleated border of a skirt or petticoat
4 Mideast leaders
5 Network of nerve cells
6 Took a chance: 2 wds.
7 One sank the Titanic
8 Cairo's river
9 "Did You Ever ____ Lassie?": 2 wds.
10 Once, once upon a time
16 ____ & AJ (teen pop band)
17 The Red or the Med
18 "____ Legend" (rock band fronted by Schuylar Croom): 2 wds.
21 Run into trouble: 3 wds.
22 Some FedEx freight: 2 wds.
23 "Frozen" reindeer
25 Indiana county
27 Ship's heading, perhaps
29 Essen exclamation
32 Find ____ for (pair with): 2 wds.
33 Peddle
34 Suffix with linguist or log
35 Bobby Brown song of 1988
36 "____ Be Me" (Jerry Lee Lewis song)
39 D.C. bigwig
40 ____ way (kind of): 2 wds.

48

Across

1. Earth
5. They usually weren't hits: hyph.
11. Donald Duck, to his nephews
12. Vexes
13. Cheat
14. Lively pieces of music
15. Model agency co-founder: 2 wds.
17. Change gear in a vehicle
18. Fort Bliss city: 2 wds.
21. Smooth
25. Chou En-___
26. "All-American Girl" Margaret
27. "Every ___ Tiger" (Tom Clancy title): 2 wds.
29. Stamp, as a document
32. Connie's portrayer, in "The Godfather"
34. Early 20th-century depiction of the ideal woman: 2 wds.
39. "Lux aeterna" composer György
40. "Men of a Certain Age" star Richard
41. Spiritual knowledge
42. "Heavens to Betsy!"
43. Jean-Paul who wrote "Being and Nothingness"
44. Sleep roughly, in British slang

Down

1. Certain
2. "The ___ Love" (R.E.M. song): 2 wds.
3. Suffix with canon or comic
4. San Diego suburb: 2 wds.
5. Turkish bath-house
6. Take a whiff of
7. Bars of gold or silver
8. Gloomy
9. "Brown ___ Girl" (Van Morrison hit)
10. Draft org.
16. Hesitant syllables
18. American ___, state tree of North Dakota
19. When doubled, a Teletubby
20. Wrestling win
22. Flying expert
23. FDR home loan org.
24. U.S. currency unit: abbr.
28. Most optimistically: 2 wds.
29. Kay Thompson character
30. "Children of the Albatross" author
31. Drooped
33. Up and about
34. "Sesame Street" veterinarian
35. "Young Frankenstein" assistant
36. Othello's betrayer
37. Genetic strands, initially
38. Former Fords
39. T-shirt sizes: abbr.

49

Across

1. Not quick to catch on: var.
5. Proprietors
11. ___-bodied
12. Abominate
13. Follow-up injection: 2 wds.
15. Elderly spinster: 2 wds.
16. Discover
21. Machine's sound
25. Aquarium fish
26. "___ Man of Constant Sorrow": 3 wds.
27. German John
28. Blue cartoon figure
30. Helpers: abbr.
31. Kind of penguin
33. "Eureka!": 3 wds.
38. Modern breakfast food: 2 wds.
42. Gentle wind
43. Cottontail's tail
44. They're boring
45. Hardy character

Down

1. Actress Olivia
2. Ancient Greek coin
3. Slog
4. Subservient response: 2 wds.
5. Fatty liquid
6. Expressed
7. "If I Ruled the World" rapper
8. Addis Ababa's land: abbr.
9. Plato's "P"
10. 6-3 or 6-4, in tennis
14. Bull: prefix
17. Contented sighs
18. Cell messenger letters
19. Hair colorer
20. "Bonanza" brother
21. Smart and seasoned
22. Gold medalist in gymnastics at the 2004 Olympics
23. "It's my turn!": 2 wds.
24. Choice
29. Architectural feature
30. Egyptian, often
32. "But of course!": 2 wds.
34. Expansive
35. "___ homo"
36. Notes for those in debt, initially
37. Some explosives, initially
38. Cable inits.
39. Coffee holder
40. Classic car
41. "___-plunk"

50

Across

1 Main stem of a tree
5 Struck
10 Call from the flock
11 Avid
12 Book that has been bought by many people
14 Disturb the composure of
15 U.S. medical research agcy.
16 Increase, with "up"
20 Canceled, as of a correction or deletion
24 Speed along
25 Montezuma, e.g.
26 Accustom (to)
28 Cool
29 Iodine, chlorine, or bromine, e.g.
31 Radio and Disco, e.g.
33 Go for the gold?
34 Terminates a debate by calling for a vote
39 Way to get rid of second-hand goods: 2 wds.
41 Plant used in the making of tequila
42 River that flows through Hamburg
43 Home of the brave
44 Be a bookworm

Down

1 Hindu title of respect
2 Black cat, to some
3 Amount to make do with
4 Rapprochement
5 Boil
6 Large shopping area
7 Gives the eye
8 Course requirement?
9 Foul up
13 Sew
17 Criminal
18 Ireland, to the Irish
19 Hammer end
20 Out of reach
21 Former Russian ruler: var.
22 Volcano in Sicily
23 Enlarge
27 Teetotaler, e.g.: hyph.
30 Opposite of perigee
32 ___ metal
35 Bathe
36 Rattling sound
37 Island of Napoleon's exile
38 Future flower
39 Gangster's sidearm
40 Lady's secret, perhaps

51

Across

1   ___-daisy: hyph.
5   Chip maker ___-Lay
10   "Go, ___!"
11   Pays
13   Time ___ half: 2 wds.
14   Lack of interest
15   Code in which many Web pages are written, initially
16   Whimsical idea
17   Cries from sties
19   "Help!": 2 wds.
21   Suffix with professor
24   Soft & ___ deodorant
25   George Strait's "All My ___ Live in Texas"
27   Photog.'s item
28   Marie, e.g.: abbr.
29   Steam engine noises
31   "Fingers crossed": 2 wds.
32   Ivanhoe's love
36   Some dishes on rooftops, initially
39   2,000 pounds: 2 wds.
40   Conductor Klemperer
41   Attractively full-figured, casually
42   Light and insubstantial
43   Timeworn
44   Suggestions on food labels, initially

Down

1   2002 Winter Olympics locale
2   Bottled (up)
3   It could make you weep: 2 wds.
4   Charlotte ___, capital of the Virgin Islands
5   Heart-to-heart: 2 wds.
6   Bank takebacks, briefly
7   "___ a loss to know what to do": 2 wds.
8   Evergreen shrub
9   Roman emperor after Galba
12   Dictionary entry: abbr.
18   "Melody Maker" alternative, initially
19   Certain 1960s protesters, initially
20   Dance, e.g.
21   Tainted, especially with disease
22   W.W. I army, initially
23   T-shirt sizes: abbr.
26   "___ 'nuff!"
30   Hullabaloo
31   One way to saute: 2 wds.
32   "Frasier" character
33   "Business Goes ___ Usual" (Roberta Flack song): 2 wds.
34   Fabric
35   "Roll With Me, Henry" singer James
37   Blade brand
38   Some beans

52

The grid:

1	2	3	4	5		6	7	8	9	10
11						12				
13						14				
		15		16			17			
18	19			20		21				
22			23				24	25		
26		27		28					29	
	30			31		32				
		33			34					
35	36	37	38	39						
40		41		42			43	44		
45				46						
47				48						

Across

1. Light metallic sound
6. Preserves, as pork
11. Neighbor of Nigeria
12. W.W. II menace: hyph.
13. 1982 Michener epic
14. Carbonara or béarnaise
15. Bargain-basement
17. Blouse, e.g.
18. Destiny
20. It's topped by tape, on a tennis court
22. "Arabian Nights" name
23. Bring to an end
26. Live show
28. Hard sell, maybe
30. ___ oil
32. Willis's "___ Hard"
33. Paleozoic, for example
34. "Psycho" actress Miles
35. Resinous deposit
38. Like oak leaves
40. Cropped up
42. Bakery attraction
45. Drainage site
46. Comedy director Keenen ___ Wayans
47. Hinged door fasteners
48. Brusque

Down

1. Certain radios
2. Cool, in the 1950s
3. Not on the move
4. Area of expertise
5. Hit, in a way
6. It "kills" some people
7. Attorneys' org.
8. Boor
9. ___ Bell
10. "___ right up!"
16. DiFranco of pop
18. A long way
19. Drinks at the bar, say
21. End
23. Intrepid
24. One way out of a building: hyph.
25. Prince, e.g.
27. Don't waste
29. ___ Michele of "Glee"
31. Great Leap Forward promoter
34. Jazz label for Basie and Ellington
35. Punishment for a sailor, maybe
36. "Celeste Aida," for one
37. Bamboozles
39. Worms, frequently
41. Break bread
43. "___ Doubtfire"
44. Sailor's "sure thing!"

53

Across

1 Plane store
7 Gallery display
10 God of light
11 Boom or gaff
12 Razor sharpeners
13 "What've you been ____?": 2 wds.
14 Type of gingham
16 Oktoberfest dance
19 "What Am ____ You?" (2004 Norah Jones single): 2 wds.
20 "A Lesson From ____" (play)
21 Lower-level gods in Hinduism and Buddhism
24 It may say "stop" or "yield"
25 Agitate
26 Trunks
28 "Ninotchka" director Lubitsch
29 Pick a candidate, say
30 Former Nigerian capital
31 Good luck charm
34 Accomplished
35 Comfy: 2 wds.
39 Audiotape holder
40 Pressure: 2 wds.
41 Anomalous
42 Attached, in biology

Down

1 Consumes
2 Apropos
3 "...____ a lender be"
4 German percussion instrument
5 Top dogs
6 ____ Parks of the civil rights movement
7 Giving sanction to
8 ____-tat-tat: hyph.
9 2004 Brad Pitt film
11 Below ground
15 ____-Atlantic
16 After the hour
17 Gallimaufry
18 Traded votes in politics
22 In addition
23 Adjusts, as an alarm clock
27 "__ true!"
28 Flying high
31 Poi source
32 Lying, maybe
33 ____ fide (law)
36 Santa ____, California
37 Heavy drinker
38 NYC to Boston dir.

54

Across

1 Curve shapes
6 Southern lady
11 Biblical possessive
12 ___ flu
13 Big artery
14 Russian-born conductor Koussevitzky
15 Largest city in California: 2 wds.
17 In a cool manner
18 Like hot goods
21 Ponytail locale
25 Bumper sticker letters
26 Catering dispenser
27 Rocky peaks
29 Concealed, like someone's face
32 Spot broadcast, often
34 Inspect with close attention
39 Pamper
40 Israeli statesman, ___ Ben Gurion
41 Ski trail
42 Easel, e.g.
43 Chipped in some chips
44 How lemonade tastes

Down

1 And others, for short: 2 wds.
2 "Out!"
3 Knights' titles
4 Consist of
5 Rap session?
6 Swiss city
7 "Brideshead Revisited" author, ___ Waugh
8 Former capital of Italy?
9 Falls behind
10 Denver to Detroit dir.
16 Martini ingredient
18 Did nothing
19 "___-te-Ching"
20 Blade
22 Arctic diving bird
23 Grand ___, Nova Scotia
24 Armageddon
28 Fairy
29 Clever comment
30 During
31 Beethoven's "Moonlight ___"
33 Made a decision, as a judge
34 "Wheel of Fortune" choice
35 Dealer's price
36 First tsar of Russia 1547–84
37 Animation
38 Boating hazard
39 Place for a manicure or a massage

55

Across

1. "What ____?": 2 wds.
5. Brag
10. Copter's cousin
11. Rich tapestry
12. Hard and shrewd bargaining: 2 wds.
14. "All Things Considered" reporter Shapiro
15. Accident investigating org.
16. ____ de Cervantes, "Don Quixote" author
18. "Son of Frankenstein" blacksmith
22. Photographer Adams
24. Writer LeShan
25. Kind of nerve
27. More fitting
29. Sporty truck
30. Carpe ____ (seize all): Lat.
32. Use a stun gun
34. ____ Delacroix ("The Green Mile" protagonist)
37. Chi follower
39. Cast
40. Agent who conducts a sale by lots
43. Queen of ____ (Biblical character)
44. Nuclear fission co-discoverer Otto
45. "____ Pretty" (song from "West Side Story"): 2 wds.
46. Cholesterol varieties, initially

Down

1. Ancient British and Irish alphabet
2. Flowers, in Florence
3. Brings water to
4. Fros' mates
5. Fight
6. Bobby and Colton
7. Mecca's land, in poetry
8. Melancholy
9. Philosopher Lao-____
13. "Oedipe" composer Georges
17. Prefix meaning "one"
19. Makes progress: 2 wds.
20. Homage in verse
21. Computer file format, initially
23. Nautical shout: 2 wds.
25. Not at home
26. School grp.
28. More, in music
31. Kind of labor
33. One running the show
35. Mercedes of "Lost in Yonkers"
36. Father-and-daughter Hollywood duo
38. "Could ____ I'm Falling in Love" (The Spinners song): 2 wds.
40. Flt. gauge
41. "Weird Al" Yankovic movie
42. Chicago Blackhawks, Toronto Maple Leafs, etc.

56

Across

1 Having a curved symmetrical structure
7 27, to 3
11 Beyond expectation: 2 wds.
12 Words before "instant" and "hour": 2 wds.
13 Dealer in rare books
15 Central parts
16 Nationals grp.
17 "Best wishes!"
20 Russian fighter
21 Harder to grasp
24 Spring source
27 Baby's soft shoe
28 Suffix with auction
29 Shrimps and lobsters
32 "Let me see…"
34 Chowder morsel
35 By necessity
40 Diva Horne
41 Checkers of vital signs
42 Poehler and Grant
43 Type of fuel distilled from petroleum: 2 wds.

Down

1 Dr.'s order?
2 Harry Potter's best friend
3 Kind of computer monitor, for short
4 Processed foods manufacturer
5 Ending for Kafka or Reagan
6 Duplicitous: hyph.
7 Fig. with a diameter
8 Neither welcome nor wanted
9 Jezebel's idol
10 Feminine suffix
14 In ____ (agitated): 2 wds.
17 Catalan surrealist
18 Large number: 3 wds.
19 Suffix for pay
20 Classic British sports car
22 Wide widths, initially
23 Grammar school basics, for short
25 Indian tribe for whom a state is named
26 ____ Wafers
30 "The Taming of the Shrew" city
31 Actor Epps and others
32 Hawaiian shake?
33 Memory: prefix
36 Tubular body structure
37 Musicians based in Maryland, initially
38 Island chain?
39 Maker of Touche Éclat, initially

57

Across

1. Small meal served with alcoholic drinks
5. Scare
11. "___ Brockovich"
12. More like mortar
13. ___ beans
14. Slow movement, in music
15. Balance sheet item
16. "Cats" showstopper
17. Broadcaster
19. Short-tailed lynx
21. "The Little Red Book" writer
24. Deviation
25. "___ will be done"
27. Supplement (with "to")
28. "... ___ he drove out of sight"
29. Aid to loading a muzzle
31. Hitchcock classic
32. Intolerant
36. Conical tent: var.
39. Zebra, e.g.
40. "Once ___ a time..."
41. Kind of school
42. Captain, e.g.
43. Diminishes
44. Aims

Down

1. Blend
2. "15 miles on the ___ Canal"
3. Country, capital Harare
4. On the mother's side
5. Weapons that spray out burning fuel: hyph.
6. Equestrian
7. Mosque figure
8. "Junk begets junk" (rule in computing, initially)
9. Prince of Wales, e.g.
10. "Iliad" city
18. "Dirty" tattletale
19. "Bon voyage!"
20. Propel, in a way
21. Almond confection
22. "Much ___ About Nothing"
23. Strange
26. Talk and talk and talk
30. Turn red, perhaps
31. Laser printer powder
32. Home, informally
33. Band with the hit "Barbie Girl"
34. Beef cut
35. "The ___ of the Ancient Mariner"
37. Duck's home
38. Signs, as a contract

58

Across

1 All in ___ work: 2 wds.
6 "A Death in the Family" author James
10 Former Portuguese dependency
11 Grain husks
13 Cash alternatives: 2 wds.
15 Reached second base, in a way
16 Makes the house bigger: 2 wds.
17 Church recesses
19 At hand
22 "One Flew Over the Cuckoo's Nest" author Kesey
25 Satirical periodical since 1952: 2 wds.
28 Big Board letters
29 Bloviates
30 Really need to bathe
32 Broadcast
35 Actor Mischa ___
39 Woman's control undergarment: 2 wds.
41 John Wayne's "The Oregon ___"
42 Iranian money
43 "¿Cómo ___ usted?"
44 Verb for thou

Down

1 Ramblers, Gremlins and Hornets, initially
2 "Charlie and the Chocolate Factory" author
3 Berry in modern diet supplements
4 Spar's tip
5 Saturate, in dialect
6 F preceders
7 Former students, briefly
8 Headset, to hams
9 Prefix meaning "within"
12 ID with two dashes, initially
14 Relaxed
18 Org. whose members often strike
19 Abbr. between a first and last name, maybe
20 "The Tell-Tale Heart" author's initials
21 Commotion, to old poets
22 Christopher Carson, familiarly
23 Chemical suffix
24 Pioneering game console, for short
26 Prince Valiant's son
27 CNN host Fareed
30 "… born to ___ right!": Hamlet: 2 wds.
31 Tony winner Tharp
32 Boston or N.Y.C., e.g.: abbr.
33 Container weight
34 Genetic letters
36 Shankar of Indian theater
37 Angled annexes
38 Software installation requirement, often
40 Initially, they eagerly await your return

59

Across

1. "Great Expectations" hero
4. "Dirty dog"
7. Chemical ending
10. Egg-shaped instrument
12. Campaigner, for short
13. City in Israel
14. Eggs, in biology
15. Abominable Snowman
16. Goat's snack, in many cartoons
17. ___ case scenario
20. Didn't just aah
22. "Exodus" hero
23. Ague cousin
24. Arboreal rodent: 2 wds.
30. Point, in baseball
31. "___ rang?"
32. Brown shade
35. What "yo mama" is
37. "___ Maria"
38. Add punch to the punch
40. Ballpoint, e.g.
41. Amos Oz, for one
45. "Lord of the Rings" bad guy
46. Building where livestock are fattened up
47. "The Catcher in the ___"
48. Nautical lurch
49. A hallucinogen, initially

Down

1. Ale holder
2. Diamonds, slangily
3. Bosom buddy
4. Cat-like mammal
5. Condo, e.g.
6. It's filled at the market
7. Age
8. Stars that increase in brightness, then fade
9. Dik-dik's kin
11. Beams
17. Major event of 1812
18. Molybdenite, e.g.
19. Free from, with "of"
21. "___ Father"
23. A good time
25. Relative of "Reverend"
26. Make more specific
27. Shag rug made in Sweden
28. Eternity, seemingly
29. Carry around, as a set of golf clubs
32. Flavor
33. "___ Heartbeat" (Amy Grant hit)
34. British coins
35. "The Turn of the ___"
36. Advantage, in sports
39. Fishing, perhaps
42. Letter after kay
43. "___ Olvidados" (1950 Luis Buñuel film)
44. "___ be a pleasure!"

60

Across

1 Before, in poetry
4 Former airline letters
7 "Oedipus ___"
8 "To each ___ own"
9 Ending for capital or social
12 Deed
13 Better
15 Collected
17 "I had no ___!"
18 ___ cheese
19 Fire starter
20 What's left
23 ___ gestae
24 Proportionately: 2 wds.
26 Adept
28 Steams up
31 Indy entrant
33 Baikal is the world's deepest
34 Bearded bloomer
35 Began
37 Motor elements
39 Follow
40 Elver's elder
41 "___ dead, Jim" ("Star Trek" line)
42 Ecru, e.g.
43 Bon ___ (witticism)
44 On ___ own terms

Down

1 Desk item
2 Go back, as a hairline
3 Exceptionally good: hyph.
4 "After that …"
5 Beaujolais, e.g.
6 ___ blond
9 Daughter of Nehru: 2 wds.
10 Brouhaha
11 Butchers' offerings
14 Afflict
16 Arabic for "commander"
19 "Nothing is more despicable than respect based on ___" (Camus)
21 Live wire, so to speak
22 Samovar, e.g.
25 A fisherman may spin one
26 Come up, as a subject
27 Bill of fare
29 Barely make: 2 wds.
30 Marsh plants
32 Abbr. on a city limit sign
35 ___ O's (discontinued Post cereal)
36 "Hey there!"
38 Omega, to an electrician

61

Across

1 Titicaca, por ejemplo
5 Sum up, for short
10 Gross, in a way
11 Suffuse, as with color
13 Tubular structure in the body: 2 wds.
15 Capt.'s prediction
16 "In the Good Old Summertime" lyricist Shields
17 Prior to, poetically
18 Capital of New Hampshire
20 CNN correspondent Robertson
21 "Dangerous Angels" author Francesca ___ Block
22 Dump
23 Classic TV equine: 2 wds.
25 Charitable fraternity, initially
26 Feline line
27 Comprehend
28 Ending for second or sediment
29 Drop a hint
33 Record co. that bought Motown in 1988
34 U.K. honor
35 "Oy ___!"
36 High-speed transportation: 2 wds.
39 "1984" author
40 "Giant" author Ferber
41 "Fiddler on the Roof" matchmaker
42 Hammer end

Down

1 Mountain Community of the Tejon Pass, Calif.
2 Finnish architect Alvar ___
3 Complain
4 Bed-in for peace participant Yoko
5 Mexican muralist
6 Adjust, as text
7 "The Amazing Race" broadcaster
8 Hall of "Martial Law"
9 Immature and silly
12 Campaign poster plea
14 Automaton, briefly
19 Lower corner of a sail
22 Computer image file format
23 Planet near the Sun
24 Majestic pronoun: 2 wds.
25 Spawn, as offspring
26 Cuban dance
27 Understated
29 Make iron into steel
30 Circumvent
31 English Channel feeder
32 1979 Alda senatorial role
37 Football great Dawson
38 Agent, briefly

62

Across

1 Bad-mouth
4 Aquatic shocker
7 Piece of equipment for a rock band: abbr.
10 Application question, often
11 ___ Day
12 Road, in Rome
13 Distance from one side to the other
16 Creep
17 Eastern wrap: var.
18 Morality subject
21 "Fudge!"
22 Like some muscles
24 Hood's gun, shortly
25 Merry-go-round
28 "Catch-22" pilot
29 Certain pickle
30 G.M. or G.E.
32 Slightest amounts
36 Skoal, e.g.
38 Links rental
39 Better-known name of Phoebe Moses: 2 wds.
42 Broccoli or spinach, for short
43 Juliet, to Romeo
44 Bud
45 "Able was I ___ ..."
46 "Don't give up!"
47 Downed a sub, say

Down

1 Flax-like fiber
2 "The X-files" extra
3 Dilly
4 Australian non-flyer
5 Audience
6 Caustic cleaners
7 Garden-variety
8 Quartz or borax, e.g.
9 Clear
14 Bake in individual dishes, as eggs
15 "Cheap" satire magazine
19 128 cubic feet
20 Mar
23 Christmas
25 Bing Crosby, for one
26 Bracket
27 Remiss
28 Harmonious interval
31 Telepathy, e.g.
33 Minute floating marine creature
34 Milk-Bone biscuit, e.g.
35 Do a do
37 Makeup, e.g.
40 "___ Gang"
41 "___ calls?"

63

Across

1 Convulsive movement
6 Rehan, Lovelace and others
10 Close-fitting outer garment
11 Roman Catholic frat. org.: 3 wds.
12 Temper, as metal
13 Stock car racer Conley
14 "___ won't be afraid" ("Stand by Me" lyric): 2 wds.
15 Average: abbr.
17 Great deal
18 Cable choice, for short
19 Ocean-going craft: 2 wds.
21 Filly
23 Pig noses
24 Center X or O
26 Country that borders Lux.
27 Ruined
30 "ER" doctor
33 Parallel
35 U.N. agency
36 Plains city, for short
37 Letters after the price of a used car
38 Middleman: abbr.
39 Garden tool
41 Withdraw as a judge
43 Holly
44 Babylonian love goddess
45 Trig function
46 Remains

Down

1 County in northwestern California
2 Very frightened: hyph.
3 Devoured dinner
4 J.C. Penney rival
5 Free-for-alls
6 Dog breeder's org.
7 Sign up for battle: 5 wds.
8 Not sinking
9 Odors
10 Ear part
16 Band of baddies
20 ___ War
22 Marionette man Tony
25 Common: prefix
27 New Zealand natives
28 Base that dissolves in water
29 Random wreckage
31 Spicy dips
32 More tender
34 Accomplishes, in the past
40 Program file extension
42 Half a dance step

64

Across

1 Canned ham glaze
6 Magicians' rods
11 Negation mark in logic
12 Require salting, maybe: 2 wds.
13 Elevate
14 Skin (suffix)
15 Bait
17 Band's vehicle, often
18 ____ Lanka (Asian island nation)
20 "The Faerie Queene" division
22 Traveled over water, in a way
24 Part of Marty Feldman's Igor costume
27 Palatal pendant
28 Amount-and-interval numbers
29 Moore of "Disclosure"
30 Has faith in
31 One over par in golf
33 "... seen nothin' ____"
34 Sun, to Domingo
36 Bridge positions
38 Beyond's partner
40 Good thing to buy in Monopoly
43 Loudness units
44 Alpha's opposite
45 Maze wall, sometimes
46 Brit's service discharge

Down

1 Absorbed, as a loss
2 Deep-____ (get rid of)
3 Pale hair color: 2 wds.
4 Between assignments
5 Order of whales and dolphins
6 Gain some unnecessary weight
7 Crack pilot
8 Body network sending signals: 2 wds.
9 Russian assembly
10 Attention ____
16 Blue
18 Ballistic missile not known for its accuracy
19 Top review
21 Old-school word for "you"
23 A little of this and a little of that
25 Allocate, with "out"
26 "Hey ... over here!"
28 Without getting one's footwear wet: hyph.
30 Cha, in England
32 "Silly" birds
34 Obi, e.g.
35 "An ill wind that nobody blows good"
37 Big book
39 ____ out (really relax, in slang)
41 I, to Claudius
42 "Frankenstein" setting

65

Across

1. Large number
5. Mississippi city, birthplace of Elvis Presley
11. Bogeyman
12. Dodger
13. Holler
14. Leave in a hurry: 2 wds.
15. Act like
16. 1952 Winter Olympics city
17. ABC News reporter Potter
18. Frightened
22. Bunk
24. Hot stuff
25. Cashless deal
27. Southern lady's salutation, stereotypically
28. Caulking fiber
30. Interval
31. Of no value
33. Go with the flow, perhaps
36. "National Velvet" author Bagnold
37. Kind of deposit
38. Court contest
41. "It's so sad!"
42. Heathers
43. On or to the left prefix
44. To wit
45. Bit to split

Down

1. Martin's "Laugh-In" partner
2. Wide open
3. Donut, e.g.: 2 wds.
4. No. on a business card
5. Not windy
6. Palatal pendants
7. Complete view
8. Tokyo, once
9. Money in Moldova
10. Crumb
16. "How ___ Has the Banshee Cried" (Thomas Moore poem)
19. French bean variety
20. Stars and Stripes land, shortly
21. Break out
23. Plenty
25. Paltry amount
26. Is in the past?
29. Drudgery doer
30. Hallucinogen's initials
32. Spacek of "Carrie"
34. "Good job!"
35. Broom made of twigs
38. King's equal in blackjack
39. Hunk of history
40. Takeaway game
41. King preceder: 2 wds.

66

Across

1 High card
4 Where people shape up
7 Matter for a judge
10 Photographer Goldin
11 Not square
12 Controversial situations, colloquially: 2 wds.
15 Pleasant way to walk: 2 wds.
16 Code name
17 Govt. property org.
18 Pick, with "for"
19 Say something
21 Odd-numbered page
24 Give weapons to
25 Reporter's question
26 African antelope
29 Make twisty
31 Scand. land
32 Didn't hold color
33 Madrid's country
35 Gas that's element #18
38 Tremendous
40 Material to be refined
41 Food container
42 "Stupid me!"
43 Needlefish
44 "Doesn't matter to me"

Down

1 Polar jacket
2 Persian or Egyptian Mau
3 Make beloved
4 Treated unfairly
5 Bakers' wares
6 Abbey area
7 Sorority letter
8 Period in the earth's history
9 Theater employee: 2 wds.
13 Tower site
14 Drink like a fish
19 ___ Francisco
20 Be nosy
22 High craggy hill
23 Brainy-looking bird
27 Butcher's cut
28 Tincture for bruises
29 Like some old photos
30 D.E.A. agent
33 E.P.A. concern
34 Prefix with graph
36 The Plastic ___ Band
37 Math degree
39 It keeps you cool in summer

67

Across

1. Boor
4. Window hangings
10. ___ of Evil
12. Aggregate
13. Exec's note
14. Exposure unit?
15. False start?
17. ___ down (sheds weight)
19. Chemistry suffix
22. Louisville Slugger, e.g.
24. Karlsbad, for one
25. "… borrower ___ a lender be"
26. Sartre's "The Transcendence of the ___"
27. Keats's "still unravish'd bride of quietness"
28. Sporty British car, for short
29. Attention
30. "I told you so!"
31. "I get it now!" sounds
32. Before, before
33. Emerson's "Circles," for instance
35. Layers
38. African trip
43. Alpine transport: hyph.
44. Slowly, to a conductor
45. Meager
46. Infatuated with: 2 wds.
47. "Tarzan" star Ron

Down

1. Place for a tent
2. Cancels
3. Place to buy cheap goods: 2 wds.
4. ___ chamber, for deep-sea divers
5. Cell stuff, initially
6. Bank letters
7. Quiche, e.g.
8. Blow one's lines, e.g.
9. View from the deck, perhaps
11. Aretha's genre
16. Neglect
18. Least crazy
19. Delightful
20. Wyle of "ER"
21. Units of energy
22. Answering machine sound
23. Biology lab supply
34. "The Seven Lively ___" (Gilbert Seldes)
36. Detective, at times
37. Ground force
38. Lack muscle tone, perhaps
39. "Without further ___ …"
40. Ardent admirer
41. "The ___ of Innocence"
42. "___ Bravo" (John Wayne film)

68

Across

1 Ball girls?
5 Old counter
11 Baseball's Hershiser
12 Everlasting, to the bard
13 Everywhere at once
15 Dabbling duck
16 Comic strip cry
17 ___ the other: 2 wds.
18 Evening hour, in Madrid
19 "___ XING" (street sign)
20 Completely: 2 wds.
23 Peacenik's phrase: 2 wds.
24 Frozen cause of water blockage: 2 wds.
26 AOL alternative
29 Brit. decorations
30 Toothpaste advertised by Bucky Beaver in the 1950s
32 O.T. book, for short
33 Election loser: hyph.
35 Soldier's award
37 Sonnet section
38 Drug carrier across the border
39 Black Sea port
40 "Grand" ice cream maker

Down

1 "Duke of Earl" or "Book of Love," stylistically: hyph.
2 Regal fur
3 On ___ knee (proposing marriage, perhaps)
4 County next to Mayo
5 Prefix with -drome
6 Bingo call: 2 wds.
7 1950s political inits.
8 Tapestry yarn
9 Detach with a hammer's claw
10 Actor Green and author Godin
14 Sentence stopper
18 Big ___, Calif.
21 Dr. Dre's old group
22 Starve
23 Super ___ (GameCube predecessor)
24 Gave out
25 Consisting of large grains or particles
26 Pillage and plunder
27 Tough to comb
28 1598 French edict city
29 Alcoholic, for short
31 Verse, in Paris
33 Some beers
34 "___ smile be your umbrella" (Bing Crosby): 2 wds.
36 Goals, e.g.: abbr.

69

Across

1 Peruvian monetary units

6 Make afraid

11 Shelley, for one

12 Whimperer

13 Musical work

15 Kamoze of reggae

16 Kind of feeling

17 Inc., overseas

18 Devoured

19 "How Can ___ Sure?" (hit of 1967): 2 wds.

20 They: Fr.

21 Chuck, Peter, Inger, et al.

23 Actors

24 Ad ___ per aspera (Kansas's motto)

26 ___ Valley (city near Los Angeles)

29 Treat with carbon dioxide

33 ___ mission: 2 wds.

34 Internet protocol inits.

35 Indian state, capital Panaji

36 "Lodi" band, for short

37 Dogfight participant

38 Early hrs.

39 Feature of many apartments

42 Merman or Mertz

43 Certain doctorate, shortly

44 Dabbling ducks

45 TDs and interceptions

Down

1 Party

2 Tooth: prefix

3 More like mortar

4 Sixth-sense letters

5 Cheap cigars

6 Maliciousness

7 Make an incision

8 Jodie Foster's birth name

9 Adds more lubricant

10 Frank's partner in the comics

14 Matter with uniform properties

22 Style of music, a fusion of Arabic and Western elements

23 Vauxhall, e.g.

25 Forwards an e-mail

26 Electrical device

27 Stir up

28 TV host Stewart

30 First name in mysteries

31 Chickadee, e.g.

32 Stands for paintings

34 Arlene and Roald

40 Disney collectible

41 Clearblue competitor

70

Across

1 Pan used in China
4 Extreme wrath
7 Complimentary poem
10 Mock, in a way
11 Edit out
12 Blend
13 Light snack or drink
16 Bishop's subordinate
17 Nautical adverb
18 ____ Jessica Parker
19 Common refrigerant
20 Hindu sacred text
22 Batman villain King ____
23 Movie actors' auditions: 2 wds.
27 Chinese principle
28 Boor's lack
29 Admits
31 Rich soil component
35 Tiny bit
36 Du Barry or Tussaud
37 Common condiment
39 Bard's "before"
40 Curved shape
41 Trade-promoting UN agcy.
42 Part of A.A.R.P.: abbr.
43 Golf ball support
44 U.S.S.R. successor

Down

1 Bends out of shape
2 "La Bohème," e.g.
3 Drink made from fermented cow's milk
4 Polar layers: 2 wds.
5 Junkyard corruption
6 Numerical suffix
7 Brunch fare
8 Eat at a restaurant: 2 wds.
9 Scopes or limits
14 Pillage, old-style
15 Blemish
19 "Not likely!": 2 wds.
21 CSI lab stuff
23 Speech disorder
24 Roe of sturgeon
25 Plant's tiny anchor
26 Musical composition
30 Drenched
32 Wizardry
33 Category of taste in food
34 Lord's workers
36 Gooey ground
38 Winery container

74

71

Across

1 Blessing
8 Nearer the source of a stream
9 Dress (up)
12 Kind of cat
13 Be in the red
14 Stomach, slangily
15 Sharp hooked claws
17 1935 Triple Crown winner, or a city
20 Takes to the prom, e.g.
21 Play place
23 "Comin' ___ the Rye"
24 Inactivity
26 Buffet
28 Not set
30 Deadly snake
32 Hullabaloos: hyph.
34 Do-nothings
36 Crank
37 Elder elver
38 He uttered "Open Sesame!": 2 wds.
41 Like some martinis
42 Fencing thrusts
43 Furtiveness

Down

1 Enthusiasm
2 Poppies' drugs
3 In a theatrical way
4 Actor Alastair
5 Major figure in "Paradise Lost"
6 Birth place
7 Great fear
9 With force and ferocity: 3 wds.
10 Dog's master
11 Bas-relief medium
16 Barrio resident
18 Purse item, briefly
19 Well-kept secret, for some
22 Blow it
25 Ancient Egypt's King ___, for short
26 Went downhill
27 Harmony
29 "Absolutely!": 2 wds.
31 Links hazards
33 Cash cache
35 Bed support
39 Furiousness
40 Car protector

72

Across

1. Chilean range
6. Enlarge: 2 wds.
11. "No ___ Bob!"
12. Beau
13. Edwin with the 1970 #1 hit "War"
14. Eyes
15. ___ Haven, CT
16. Astronomer Bart
18. "Argo" director Affleck
19. ___ Lanka
20. Groenland, par exemple
21. Bathroom, in Bristol
22. Amateur sports grp.
24. Fam. tree member
25. Append: 2 wds.
27. De ___
28. In the past, in the past
29. Red or Brave, for short
30. "Take a chair!"
31. Washington, e.g.: abbr.
32. Ben-Hur was chained to one
35. Est., once
36. "Bah!"
37. 157.5 degrees from N.
38. Military camp
40. Figure skater Cohen
42. Disorderly
43. "On ___ to know basis": 2 wds.
44. Aides: abbr.
45. Billiard shot

Down

1. Clubs: abbr.
2. Fertilizer component
3. Way to randomly choose a person for an unpleasant task: 2 wds.
4. Always, in verse
5. Like tennis star Novak Djokovic
6. Came to
7. Disney dwarf
8. Betrays: 2 wds.
9. Bony fish
10. River to the Atlantic
17. Motor suffix, commercially
23. Army bed
24. Actor Daniel ___ Kim
25. Mosaic piece
26. British blue-bloods: abbr.
27. Refuse
29. "The Matrix" hero
31. "___ Anatomy"
33. "Angela's ___" (1996 best seller)
34. Aptly named English novelist
39. May hrs., in Modesto
41. Gasteyer formerly of "SNL"

73

Across

1 Travel around making political speeches
6 Expanse of short grass
11 Jay Silverheels's role, once
12 Gay place
13 Burnett and Brockovich
14 Original "Battlestar Galactica" commander
15 Hosp. employee
16 Professor's helpers, shortly
18 Bristol-Myers roll-on brand
19 River islet
20 Periodic table suffix
21 "And ____ my cap": 2 wds.
22 Shoulder muscles, briefly
24 Maui tourist destination
25 Uses for support: 2 wds.
27 Like a desert
29 Bridle straps
31 Shiba ____, Japanese breed of dog
32 ____ Cruces, N.M.
33 Of a thing
35 Measure of an economy, initially
36 They protect QBs
37 Miracle-____ (plant fertilizer)
38 Insane, slangily
40 "Men ____ Life" (Warhol painting): 2 wds.
42 Regions
43 Blender brand
44 Beaver's den
45 Foul

Down

1 Gravestone, perhaps
2 Inactive, apathetic
3 Having undisturbed continuity
4 Range part: abbr.
5 Messages that stick: hyph.
6 Hiccup, for instance
7 Big roll of cash
8 Tales of Middle Eastern origin: 2 wds.
9 Refuse to leave
10 "Star Trek" empath Troi
17 Of the southern hemisphere
23 Author Harper
24 ____ polloi (common people)
26 Therapy period
27 Apparatus on a railroad
28 Long-distance vehicle race over rough terrain
30 Highway
32 ____-leaf binder
34 Contrite
39 Depression
41 Hush-hush D.C. org.

74

Across

1 Ghastly
8 Show signs of age, as a roof
11 Horse noted for intelligence, grace, and speed
12 Abbr. at the top of sheet music
13 Umpire's shout before "You're out!": 2 wds.
15 Private pupil
16 Threadbare
17 "___ Tú" (Mocedades hit)
18 Types
19 Currency unit of the U.S.
20 Missouri natives
21 Ashtray things
22 River formations
24 Actress Sue ___ Langdon
27 Calling
28 Before: abbr.
29 Imminent, old-style
30 Baseball manager Joe
31 Kids' TV network
33 Summer setting letters
34 Overhead photos
35 Circus cries
36 Karen's maid on "Will & Grace"

Down

1 Like sailing ships
2 Conductor Toscanini
3 Syndicate
4 "___ Irish Rose"
5 Kid transport
6 "Commando's" ___ Dawn Chong
7 Petitions
8 Jean-Paul who wrote "Words are loaded pistols"
9 Alpine ridges
10 "___ Anatomy" (ABC offering)
14 Executes, in a way
18 The Sun, for example: 2 wds.
20 Canal locale: 2 wds.
21 Cheerless
22 Breakfast item
23 Builds
24 Overdue sum
25 ___ oil (cologne ingredient)
26 "True enough, but…": 2 wds.
27 "No problemo": 2 wds.
28 Declamation stations
30 High spots
32 "Seinfeld" uncle

75

Across

1 Switch from paper to plastic, say

6 Fruit used in Caribbean cookery: var.

11 Teaser: abbr.

12 Brave

13 Gadget, slangily

14 Have ___ for (be perceptive to): 2 wds.

15 Awesome: 2 wds.

17 Business execs in charge of accounts, initially

19 Suffolk, for one, in Shakespeare

20 Former name of the cable network Versus, initially

21 Fixers

24 Campaign pro.

25 Prone

26 "Tru ___!"

27 Language of Stockholm

29 Brit. honor, initially

30 Carry

31 "The Hunger Games" fan, probably

32 Among other things: 2 wds.

35 Hopeless: 2 wds.

36 Circle

39 Castilian hero: 2 wds.

40 Gently and sweetly, in music

41 Composer Saint-___

42 Start of a clairvoyant's comment, perhaps: 3 wds.

Down

1 "Dark Souls," e.g.

2 Verdi's "___ tu"

3 Salad ingredient: 2 wds.

4 Tracers, bullets, etc.

5 Gunk

6 Plant with showy flowers

7 Don't believe it

8 Intelligent and well informed

9 "If all ___ fails…"

10 Close looker

16 Far from the surface of the ocean: hyph.

17 Officers, casually

18 Uninterrupted stream or discharge

21 Head waiters, for short: 2 wds.

22 "Streamers" playwright

23 "Nana" star Anna

28 Kills, slangily: 2 wds.

31 Early weather satellite, initially

32 Chemical suffixes

33 Italian city in Campania, Italy

34 City and commune in Lombardy, northern Italy

37 Rink surface

38 It may be high in the afternoon

Across

1 U.S. Army medal
4 Relative of "Reverend"
7 1860s inits.
10 Tolkien cannibal
11 Number worn by Lionel Messi
12 Parrot's cry
13 Nicaragua monetary unit
15 "Vive le ___!"
16 Israeli oil port: var.
17 Trinidadian musician and bandleader Edmundo
18 "Cola Wars" side
21 Archeological site
23 River to the North Sea
24 Prefix meaning "one-billionth"
25 Know-it-all
29 Fund-raising grps.
30 "Dead Poets Society" director Peter
31 Seeming
33 Doesn't eat, for religious reasons
34 Hooded snake
35 Iago, notably
37 Golf peg
38 Fed juice to?
42 Swiss river
43 BBC rival
44 Devon river
45 Online feed, initially
46 "If I Ruled the World (Imagine That)" rapper
47 Coxcomb

Down

1 Wyatt's cohort
2 "No more seats," briefly
3 "Up Around the Bend" band, briefly
4 Popular vodka, briefly
5 "___: My Story": C&W autobiography
6 Caught: 3 wds.
7 Los ___, Spain
8 Faint
9 "___ Before Dying": 2 wds.
14 Abandons
18 Latin foot
19 Blight victim
20 "I Spent My Summer Vacation Rolling a 300" and such?
22 Napping, so to speak
24 Governed by Cuomo, initially
26 Cello elevator
27 Small bird
28 Fourth-year high school students: abbr.
31 Doha's land
32 "___ directed" (medicine alert): 2 wds.
33 Babes in the woods
36 Bit
39 Football official, for short
40 Outer: prefix
41 Passbook abbr.

77

Across

1 Earthlink competitor, initially
4 Some linemen, in football, initially
7 Passage
9 Metric measurements: abbr.
12 It'll cure anything
13 Sigh of release
14 Alternatives to plasma TVs
15 Daughter of Zeus
17 Crook's other name
19 Ink ingredient
20 Desire
21 Russian horseman
23 More soiled
25 Cultivated
27 Blvds.
30 Be
31 Modern letters: hyph.
33 Coined money
35 Four-time Pro Bowl tight end Crumpler
36 One-time domestic flight co.
37 A way the wind blows
39 Runway guess, for short
40 Madonna's daughter
41 Like 24 of the words in this puzzle: abbr.

Down

1 Amusing oneself: 2 wds.
2 Delphic medium
3 Airstrip: 2 wds.
4 U.S. Army medal
5 "___ Yellow Ribbon Round the Ole Oak Tree" (song): 2 wds.
6 The U.S. as seen from abroad
8 Rocket launcher, initially
9 Dish created by Mexican restaurateur Cardini: 2 wds.
10 Bouncing off the walls
11 Hit a golf ball wrong, sometimes
16 Engine attachment
18 Scarcely detectable amount
22 "Take Me Bak ___" (1972 Slade song)
24 Computer acronym
25 View for a further time
26 An exiled American, shortly
28 Big cat in Caen
29 Coasters
32 Bryn ___, college in Pennsylvania
34 Civil Rights Act grp.
38 Pol., Port., etc.

78

Across

1 Dried coconut meat
6 Willow
11 Brine-cured cheeses
12 Apartment that's owned, not leased
13 Made an emergency set-down: 2 wds.
15 It can be spent in Naypyidaw
16 Super-duper: hyph.
17 Becomes solid, like concrete
20 Nonetheless
22 Not just my or your
23 Put in order
27 Motion onward
29 Uncomfortable position: 2 wds.
30 11th of 12: abbr.
31 Smidgen
32 Go against
33 Lasting impression
36 It may be fragile
38 Mood lightener: 2 wds.
43 Combat zone
44 Not a soul: 2 wds.
45 Like stray dogs
46 Made level

Down

1 Ozone depleter, shortly
2 Above, in poems
3 Money-raising grp.
4 Scratches
5 Like an old grate
6 Spanish goose
7 Classical compositions
8 Prefix with European
9 Biblical garden site
10 Went on a boat or a plane
14 Church figure: 2 wds.
17 Jr., last year
18 Continental currency
19 Horse's gait
21 Formerly, in olden days
23 Community
24 Between eight and ten
25 Bobble
26 Deadly sin
28 Minimal wear item: hyph.
32 Sorrow
33 Ponzi scheme, e.g.
34 Mrs. Dithers in "Blondie"
35 "I'll second that"
37 Lady's man
39 Coral reef
40 Slip in a pot, initially
41 NYC to Boston dir.
42 Gave grub to

79

Across

1. Composed
6. ___ Lee cakes
10. Big house occupant?
11. Sink fitting: hyph.
12. "Is that good ___?": 2 wds.
13. Suffix for di or pan
14. TV show set in Massachusetts: 2 wds.
16. "___, you noblest English!": 2 wds.
17. Composer Kern
21. Amorphous food
25. Tiny time unit: abbr., 2 wds.
26. South Seas starch
27. Mil. prep. course
28. Pakistani city
30. Eye askance
32. Changing digits
39. German town
40. Fur source
41. Eye sores
42. Actress Téa
43. Briny bodies
44. Nothing to it: 2 wds.

Down

1. Messy dresser
2. Novice
3. F-16's homes, initially
4. "___ my peas with honey…": 2 wds.
5. Archenemy of the Fantastic Four: 2 wds.
6. Intensity
7. As limp as ___: 2 wds.
8. Hindu deity
9. "Come on, be ___!": 2 wds.
11. Ball-and-mallet game
15. Hurricane dir.
17. Dad's namesake: abbr.
18. That, in Tijuana
19. Done working: abbr.
20. Blocks
22. "7 Faces of Dr. ___"
23. Hockey legend Bobby
24. "The Bells" poet
28. Med. country
29. Anatomical ring
31. Ambulance staffers, for short
32. Blog feeds, initially
33. Major ending?
34. Bottled spring water brand
35. Hwys.
36. Have ___ good authority: 2 wds.
37. 1980s German pop star
38. Film crew member

80

Across

1 Olden drum
6 Garbage
11 In the know
12 Perfume
13 "At the Center of the Storm" author George
14 Bus alternatives
15 Campus quarters
17 Dermatologist's concern
18 Clover site
20 Bounce, as from a bar
22 Sea eagles
24 "Memoirs of a ___" (Arthur Golden novel)
28 Certain fraction
30 Manages
31 Bracing coastal atmosphere: 2 wds.
33 Stoolie
34 Cold cuts, e.g.
36 Good buddies use them, initially
37 0.5 fl. oz.
40 Bit
42 Put in the cup
44 Having a cupola
47 Gloss over, like a syllable
48 Wing-shaped
49 "Ahoy ___!"
50 Dive (for)

Down

1 Body art, for short
2 Cause of speechlessness
3 Colorful neckerchief: var.
4 100+-year-old cookie
5 Backward-looking, in fashion
6 Avena sativa grain
7 Half or quarter, e.g.
8 Cunning
9 "The Folks That Live On The Hill" author
10 Endure
16 Coffee holder
18 Contact, e.g.
19 Shallowest of the Great Lakes
21 Part of a min.
23 Rush of frightened animals
25 Astronaut
26 Basil, e.g.
27 Calls for
29 Get going
32 Aries animal
35 ___ wave (tsunami)
37 Opponents of "us"
38 Gaucho's weapon
39 Open, as an envelope
41 Balsam used in perfumery
43 "L.A. Law" actress Susan
45 Unit of energy
46 Make a different color, like hair

81

Across

1. Rocker Bob
6. City in Mercer County, Illinois
11. ___ orange
12. Cut into cubes
13. Method used for long print runs
15. Commonly: 2 wds.
16. "The Ballad of ___" Tennyson poem
17. Fix firmly: var.
19. Beginning stage of a study: 2 wds.
22. European fish
25. Of Europe, Asia, etc.
28. 1960s campus grp.
29. In a rush
30. Slaver
32. Early stage of life
35. Breaks down, in a way
39. Alcoholic drink: 3 wds.
41. Frosted
42. End of ___: 2 wds.
43. Hodgepodges
44. One of 150 in the Bible

Down

1. Short-billed rail
2. Class for foreigners, for short
3. Cat, in Catalonia
4. Self-centered person
5. Grade at a gas station: abbr.
6. On ___ (how some pranks are performed): 2 wds.
7. Enraged
8. O.A.S. member: abbr.
9. Actress Laura of "Rambling Rose"
10. Greek theaters
14. Fabled outlaw: 2 wds.
18. "Kill Bill" tutor Pai ___
19. Compaq products, initially
20. Mortar porter
21. Reply to a ques.
22. "Is ___?": 2 wds.
23. "From ___ even to Beersheba": Judges
24. Taina of "Les Girls"
26. Letters that end "Old MacDonald Had a Farm"
27. "Ozzie and Harriet" family
30. Harsh Athenian lawgiver
31. Hall of Famer Sandberg et al.
32. Breakfast brand
33. Flour-grinding place
34. ___ B'rith
36. Highest draft rating: hyph.
37. Engage in logrolling
38. Get-rich-quick idea
40. Touch on the shoulder

82

Across

1. Chip in passports, initially
5. Not go to bed: 2 wds.
11. One from Hanover
12. Country with a canal
13. Mardi ___
14. Mt. ___ (where Noah landed)
15. Ending for capital or social
16. "The Thin Man" canine
17. Indifferent individual
19. Major can maker
23. E.R. workers
24. Gaucho's rope
25. As blind as ___: 2 wds.
27. Computer screens, briefly
28. ___ Works (Monopoly utility)
30. "There's no ___ T-E-A-M": 2 wds.
31. Wipe clean
32. Indian corn
35. Fill-in: abbr.
37. US radio service, initially
38. Discord
41. Far-extending
42. Hair color
43. Asia's shrinking ___ Sea
44. Changes
45. Ashen

Down

1. "Million Dollar Password" host Philbin
2. Leading the pack
3. Juliet, to Romeo
4. ___ Moines, Ia.
5. Healthful retreats
6. It can cause tooth decay
7. "Falcon Crest" actress: 2 wds.
8. Shostakovich's "Babi ___" Symphony
9. John's "Pulp Fiction" co-star
10. Butter serving
16. Summer coolers, for short
18. Part of the alimentary canal
20. Meat-eating order of mammals
21. Mel of baseball fame
22. Some batteries, initially
25. Cow, maybe
26. Rule out
29. Cold freight car
30. Devilish type
33. Like some defensive strategies
34. Bald bird
36. Subway Series team
38. Govt. agency founded in 1953, initially
39. One-time MTV afternoon show
40. Furrow
41. Race unit

83

Across

1 Cleaning cloths
5 Refuse to speak: 2 wds.
11 Fairy tale villain
12 Spin
13 Horn sound
14 Orbital high point
15 Place for pollen
17 Evasive
19 Butts into
22 Feel similarly
23 Remiss
25 J.F.K. regulators
26 Bleed
27 Long stories
30 Alternative to glue
32 Chemical compound suffix
33 Invective
34 Turkey wattle
36 Over there
39 Inclines
42 Change gradually
43 Smooth
44 Cotton fabric with a shiny finish
45 Narrow opening

Down

1 Poppycock
2 Before now
3 Heavy, ribbed fabric
4 Small sofa
5 Jam-pack
6 Runners
7 Not harmonic, like music
8 Kind of wheels
9 Adaptable truck, for short
10 ___ Dee River
16 Sailor's assent
17 Espresso stop
18 Visibly astonished
20 Kangaroo or wombat
21 Rabbits' tails
24 Patella's place
28 Pamper
29 Shirt part
30 Good friend
31 Goes down
35 Birdhouse nester
36 "Sure thing!"
37 Eggs, to a scientist
38 "We are ___ amused"
40 Chi follower
41 Tennis match part

84

Across

1 "___ big deal": 2 wds.
6 Flees
10 Bogotá babies
11 Pinch sharply: 2 wds.
12 In an attractive way
14 Group founded by Daryle Jenklns, initially
15 Big picture: abbr.
16 Certain painting
17 Admonish
19 Two-year degree type
20 "Because of You" singer: hyph.
21 Ex-Yankee pitcher Hideki
23 Greek twenty prefix
25 Kind of rug
27 Took a horse
31 Actor Chaney, Jr.
32 Drive insane: 2 wds.
34 Currency exchange board, initially
35 Athenian vowel
36 Son of Gad (Genesis 46:16)
37 Equivalent
40 Tampa Bay Rays coach Baldelli
41 ___ Antoinette
42 ___'acte (break between two parts of a play)
43 Lend ___ (assist): 2 wds.

Down

1 Natural
2 Cone-shaped home
3 Irritable
4 Opposite of alt: Ger.
5 Bone: prefix
6 "Turandot" slave girl
7 Coolness and composure
8 Coconut-based rum
9 Panache
11 Eagles, Falcons and Ravens, e.g.
13 Safe from injury
18 French kings
22 River to the Rhine
24 Regained consciousness: 2 wds.
25 "What's your hurry?": 2 wds.
26 Enlist for military service
28 Golfer Mark
29 Samantha's "Bewitched" husband
30 Worked on, as a newspaper article
31 "Filthy" dough
33 Buddhist principle of causality
38 A.T.M. maker
39 Cry of disbelief

85

Across

1 Slot machine symbol
4 Anatomical pouch
7 Beer variety, initially
8 Creative drive
9 When doubled, a Teletubby
12 Poppy derivatives
14 Breed of dog, for short
15 Puncture sound
16 Blood's partner
17 "A Passage to India" heroine
19 Eyelid maladies
20 "Bleak House" girl
21 Sedate
23 J.J. Pershing's command in W.W. I
24 Different ending?
25 Bleat
28 Auto pioneer Citroën
30 Suffix with Ecuador
31 Actress Anouk
33 Geometric ratios
35 ___-a-brac
36 Art class feedback session, slangily
37 ___ Harbour, Florida
38 Followers of a Chinese philosophy
41 King in Spain
42 Enero to enero
43 "The Raven" author's monogram
44 "Kapow!"
45 Codebreaking arm of govt.

Down

1 High school class, for short
2 Software program, briefly
3 Bring up kids: 3 wds.
4 Reserves: 2 wds.
5 Gets on in years
6 Corporations: abbr.
9 Four-term senator from Texas: 2 wds.
10 Alpine river
11 Shinzo ___, prime minister of Japan
13 Be laid up
16 Volkswagen model
17 Good credit rating letters
18 Ike, initially
19 Where goods are displayed
22 Road crew supply
26 Dental org.
27 Years, to Yves
29 Japanese computer giant, initially
31 Short form, for short
32 "Dies ___"
34 It's three, on some clocks
36 Marriage site in John 2:1–11
38 Bill at a bar
39 Professor's helpers, initially
40 Facial business

86

Across

1 Agency responsible for highways, initially
5 Snare drum noise: hyph.
11 Comb. form denoting flow
12 Bring to a boil?
13 Anthropologist Fossey
14 Elephant, e.g.
15 Having no name
17 Catcall
18 Snaky swimmers
22 Bowler, for one
24 Not getting up: 2 wds.
26 Like ghost stories
28 Plant pores
29 Geometric pattern repeated at every scale
31 Dress (with "up" or "out")
32 Font contents
33 Lunch spot
35 With very little space between: hyph.
39 Historical account or biography
42 Carve in stone
43 Come about
44 Calamitous
45 Showing gentleness
46 Pond gunk

Down

1 Pakistani tongue
2 Front part of the leg
3 Structure that is very unsafe
4 "___ Kröger" (novella by Thomas Mann)
5 Investment option
6 "Dinner at the Homesick Restaurant" novelist Tyler
7 Poseidon's weapon
8 Scottish hat
9 Certain foreign dignitary
10 ___ Avivian
16 Available, in a way: 2 wds.
19 Self-centred
20 Big car for a celeb
21 Grab
22 Bulk
23 Ethereal
25 The British ___ (Great Britain, Ireland, etc.)
27 Ready to drink, like a beer: hyph.
30 Worshiper
34 English university city
36 Not pre-recorded, as a concert
37 Off-white shade
38 Opponents
39 Assembled
40 The night before
41 Back-to-work time: abbr.

87

Across

1 Cutter with a broad blade
4 "20/20" network
7 Aardvark's tidbit
10 Cousin of rage
11 One who plays for a living
12 Anonymous John
13 Calendar abbr.
14 Blood poisoning
16 Heroic poem
18 Asian persimmons
19 Second shot
21 Chemical compound suffix
23 One-eyed, long-bearded Norse god
24 Ten-cent coin
25 "2001" computer
27 Your, in the Bible
29 Salon offering
30 Beers
32 ___ Ham, London suburb
34 Delhi wrap
35 Lacking moral sense
38 Shaving need
40 "Road" film destination
41 General pardon
43 Wine cask
44 Merry mo.
45 "Titanic" actor DiCaprio
46 Like an antique
47 "___ on a Grecian Urn"
48 Eccentric
49 Beam

Down

1 Pointer
2 Hang
3 Non-acceptance of antisocial behavior: 2 wds.
4 Pertinent
5 Full of sorrow: hyph.
6 Hip joint
7 Business manager
8 Harmful
9 ___ Party Nation
15 Managed, with "out"
17 Down
20 Christopher Carson, familiarly
22 Court decision
25 Owns
26 Fearful
28 Thanksgiving side dish
31 Small, medium or large
33 Have a bawl
36 "Be-Bop-___" (1956 Gene Vincent hit): hyph.
37 Swing dance, ___ Hop
39 Munch Museum's locale
41 Time-wasting bother
42 Smallest Hebrew letter

88

Across

1 Hack
4 "Rings" found in a tree
7 Available, with "on"
10 Calif., Fla., Ill., etc.
11 Autograph seeker, perhaps
12 "___ Of Destruction"
13 Casual tops: hyph.
15 "Holy smokes!"
16 "I Saw Three Ships Come Sailing In," e.g.
17 A.T.M. need
18 Husky breaths
21 In a fitting way
23 "Surfer," so to speak
24 Eggs, to a scientist
25 Protector on the gridiron: 2 wds.
30 "Dear old" guy
31 Substantial, as a sum
32 Cash or gold coins, e.g.
35 Jenny Lind, e.g.
36 "Aren't you ___ one who always said…"
37 "Hey, what's the big ___?"
39 Once around the track
40 Music genre
44 "Wheel of Fortune" purchase: 2 wds.
45 "Slippery" tree
46 Program, for short
47 Calypso offshoot
48 Caribbean, e.g.
49 Congratulations, of a sort

Down

1 "Stop shooting!"
2 Jesus's mount, in John
3 "A Christmas Carol" outburst
4 Big dos
5 Airplane boarding place
6 Put in irons
7 Act the siren
8 Be of service to
9 Marshall of "Awakenings"
14 Gate-crash
18 Boil fluid
19 Bat wood
20 "The Matrix" role
22 Approaching but not reaching: 2 wds.
24 "That's ___ …"
26 Milky plant fluids
27 Pandowdy, e.g.
28 Annex
29 ___ job
32 Book of maps
33 Meat cut
34 Brownish pigment
35 1965 King arrest site
38 "Over" follower in the first line of "The Caissons Go Rolling Along"
41 Father, to Huck Finn
42 "Fat" farm
43 Decide to leave, with "out"

89

Across

1 Heckler's hoot
4 Country rtes.
7 Lawyer's gp.
10 Wine: prefix
11 Ample shoe width
12 "___ wise guy, eh?": 2 wds.
13 One tenth of a sen
14 Suffix with differ
15 Kind of camera, initially
16 Hawaii
19 Variety, as of an animal
20 Protective garment
23 Harder to locate
27 "Polythene ___" (Beatles song)
28 Corn holder
29 Ogee shapes
32 Bridges
34 "Blame It on Me" singer Davis
36 Drink made with cream of coconut and rum: 2 wds.
41 "___ for apple": 2 wds.
42 Alt. spelling
43 Block
44 Emeritus: abbr.
45 Before, for Burns
46 Super Bowl highlights, for many
47 Parts of finan. portfolios
48 Certain sibling, affectionately
49 Pollen carrier

Down

1 When doubled, a South Pacific island
2 Eye, to Pierre
3 "Step ___ pets" (popular palindrome): 2 wds.
4 Win back, as trust
5 Heavy, like bread
6 Irish ___ (breed of dog)
7 ___ prof.
8 Tree trunk
9 Rhine feeder
17 "Curb Your Enthusiasm" network
18 Holly Hunter in "The Piano"
20 Gorilla, e.g.
21 Dance step
22 Real estate ad abbr.
24 Camcorder brand letters
25 Long, long time
26 Tony Dorsett, John Riggins, etc.
30 Suffix with Jacob
31 Breaks one's back
32 Sleeping sounds
33 Cohort
35 Some mites
36 Motley
37 Adherents: suffix
38 Basic verse option
39 Miami-___ County
40 "As I Lay Dying" father
41 ___ welder

90

Across

1 Part of a church that contains the altar
5 Monte Carlo attraction
11 Busiest
12 Daniel Webster, for one
13 "Chariots of Fire" finale
14 Puddinglike dessert
15 Be at fault
16 Revolved
17 Goo
19 Brown ermine
23 "Crouching Tiger, Hidden Dragon" director
24 Like "Lost" episodes
25 "For Your ____ Only"
27 "__, please" ("I like mine still mooing")
28 Igneous rock, originally
30 Chicken Little's mother, e.g.
31 ____ shooting
32 ____ Allan Poe
35 Lion's "meow"
37 Major time period
38 Star sign
41 Chum, e.g.
42 Taken
43 Empty
44 Lets out, say
45 "Story of My Life" Mike

Down

1 ____-ski
2 Steinbeck opus, with "The"
3 Gross irreverence
4 Barely get, with "out"
5 Provide for free, informally
6 Incite, as passion
7 Strolled
8 "____ just what I wanted!"
9 #s
10 State that "Portlandia" is filmed in: abbr.
16 "Get it?"
18 Spellbind
20 Citrus drink
21 "____ Force One" (1997 Harrison Ford film)
22 Driving need
25 Common couple?
26 Animal whose name also means "to talk nonstop"
29 Penitent
30 "____ Town Too" (1981 hit)
33 Seed coverings
34 Gives a five, maybe
36 Assists
38 Fed. construction overseer
39 "Electric" creature
40 Cambridge sch.
41 Recycling ____

91

Across

1 Musical "repeat" sign

6 Homes for doves

11 Roots used in the Hawaiian dish poi

12 "Two Women" star

13 Golf bag items

14 Midwest hub

15 Modern-sounding creature?

16 Letters seen in red, white and blue

18 Old style "For shame!"

19 Door sign

20 Arctic bird

21 Casbah headgear

22 Venomous snakes

24 Not looking good, to say the least

25 What a crossword clue might be

27 A lot of ice

29 Puts up

32 Director ___ Howard

33 Hereditary material, initially

34 Actor Holm

35 "Them!" creature

36 Bizarre

37 Bar order

38 Compassion

40 Cry of surrender

42 Leave via ladder, maybe

43 Amber or umber

44 Singer Bob

45 Decorative jugs

Down

1 Bad mark

2 Made, as money

3 "___ to Major Tom …" Bowie line

4 ___ compos mentis

5 Urn for bones

6 Disguise

7 "Amazing!"

8 Road junction with a central island: 2 wds.

9 More inexplicable

10 Need a tissue

17 Dangle, hang

23 "___ Time transfigured me": Yeats

24 Boneshaker's cube

26 Slander

27 Incriminated, set up

28 Deserted

30 Former U.S. president Zachary

31 Bad looks

33 Experienced leader

39 Bean counter, for short

41 "Right this instant!"

92

Across

1 Pre-Revolution leaders
6 Inflatable trait
9 Pierces
12 Grass's morning cover
13 Hardy cattle breed
14 Motor lodge
15 Head protrusion
16 "How I Met Your Mother" network
17 Enemy
18 Strive
19 Stranger, more eccentric, slangily
21 Chop down
22 Eliot or Loch
23 Next to
26 Clip at
27 Groove
28 Mentor
30 Historic beginning
33 Author of "The Tell-Tale Heart"
34 Scottish cap
35 Hit head-on
36 In favor of
37 Completely idiotic
39 Historian's period
40 Put under a military blockade
41 N. ___ (st. whose capital is Bismarck)
42 Influential tribesperson

Down

1 Lhasa's land
2 Sling mud
3 Silly trick
4 U.K. flying corps
5 Ease off
6 Instructed for moral improvement
7 Like Columbus, by birth
8 Proprietors
10 Extra effort, figuratively: 2 wds.
11 Barely passable: hyph.
20 Make a sweater
21 Kachina doll maker
23 Principality in the Pyrenees
24 Evergreen tree of the Old South: 2 wds.
25 Conjecture
26 Drained, exhausted
29 Pierce
30 Asked nosy questions
31 Mountain group
32 High guy in Dubai: var.
38 It's nothing

93

Across

1 Kuwaiti, e.g.
5 Come-ons
11 1995 earthquake city
12 Tired person's utterance: 2 wds.
13 Emphatic type: abbr.
14 Blue
15 Vintner's prefix
16 Bass, e.g.
17 "Rebecca of Sunnybrook Farm" director Allan
19 Home of four ACC teams: abbr., 2 wds.
23 Ranch add-on
25 Milan opera house: 2 wds.
27 Hawaiian porch
29 Race of Norse gods
30 More lithe
32 "Get it?"
33 ____ -de-camp
34 Angelou or Lin
36 Univ. in Troy, N.Y.
38 ____ 'acte
41 Dr. Seuss egg hatcher
44 "Zip-____-Doo-Dah"
45 "Remington ____" (1980s show)
46 Way around London, once
47 Frozen cause of water blockage: 2 wds.
48 "The Odd Couple" director

Down

1 Sony co-founder Morita
2 Automatic
3 Left
4 In steerage, say
5 European capital
6 Actor Jannings
7 Lack
8 Et ____ (and the following): abbr.
9 ____ Claire, Wis.
10 ____-Anne-des-Plaines, Quebec
18 Came down to earth
20 Daughter of the Trojan king Priam
21 "I cannot tell ____": 2 wds.
22 Like the first issue of "Action Comics"
23 "Born Free" lioness
24 First name in raga
26 "____ Smile" (1976 hit)
28 Gave a heads-up to
31 "8 Mile" actor
35 "Sailing to Byzantium" poet
37 Silents star Negri
39 Deck material
40 Radiation dosages
41 Fu-____ (legendary Chinese sage)
42 Stock page heading, initially
43 Riddle-me-____ (rhyme)

94

Across

1 Wildebeests
5 When doubled, a Washington city
10 In ___ (hurried): 2 wds.
11 Grant-___ (government subsidy): 2 wds.
12 Hearsay: hyph.
14 Cosa ___, criminal org.
15 Fork over, with "up"
16 Original sinner
17 Army figure, for short
19 100 cts.
20 Skin: suffix
22 Principal dish of a meal
24 Having a sandy color
26 Minnesota iron ore range
28 "___ Ben Adhem" (Leigh Hunt poem)
31 F.A.A. airport service
32 Army rank, initially
34 Make a scene?
35 Chicago mayor ___ Emanuel
37 "Valse ___" (Sibelius orchestral piece)
39 Leech, e.g.
41 Loud-roaring animals of the cat family
42 As a result of: 2 wds.
43 Gulf of Aqaba port
44 Guesses, briefly

Down

1 Long, narrow depression
2 Place for young children: 2 wds.
3 DOT, alternatively
4 Having had the wool clipped off
5 "Buena Vista Social Club" director ___ Wenders
6 Relative of the buffalo
7 Hamper for dirty clothes: 2 wds.
8 Small
9 Stick
10 Bearded, as barley
13 Some "Nip/Tuck" procedures
18 Lennon's widow
21 ___ culpa
23 Air letters, once?
25 Weight abbr.
26 Monument material
27 And others: 2 wds.
29 Bands of eight
30 In ___ (like a baby, before birth)
33 Unrefined
36 "___ Lisa"
38 Critical hosp. areas, initially
40 "Spring ahead" hrs.

95

Across

1 Kind of wheel

7 Actor Hakeem ___-Kazim, Colonel Iké Dubaku in "24"

10 Go back

11 Darkens

12 Reduced, in a way: 2 wds.

13 Little bit of everything dish

14 Shared by all

16 Development area: 2 wds.

19 ___-Flush (former bathroom cleaner)

20 Made a shrill cry

24 "Over the moon," e.g.

26 Croatian leader?

27 Transgressed

29 Sculptor, painter and architect, ___ Lorenzo Bernini

30 Edge along some mountaintops

32 Early Christian church

35 One-time Tampa Bay Buccaneers tackle Jason

36 More snug

40 Together, musically: 2 wds.

41 "Ocean's ___"

42 "Kidnapped" monogram

43 Long arm of the Indian Ocean: 2 wds.

Down

1 Away, idiomatically

2 Velvet finish?

3 Candy striper's coworkers, shortly

4 Period between a stimulus and response: 2 wds.

5 Eskimo's house

6 Suitable

7 Baking locale

8 "___ Psycho" (song by Midwest rapper Tech N9ne): 3 wds.

9 Class for foreigners, for short

11 Having two layers of glass (windows): hyph.

15 Actress Marsh and others

16 Pitchfork-shaped letters

17 "___ but known...": 2 wds.

18 "Come ___!" (enter): 2 wds.

21 Toyota hybrid models

22 Abba of Israel

23 Janet Jackson's "What Have You ___ for Me Lately?"

25 European thrush

28 Windshield clearer: hyph.

31 Sorbonne, e.g.

32 Big pig

33 Extra: abbr.

34 Kind of chef

37 E.R. hookups

38 Wide shoe width

39 Biology letters

96

Across

1 "You ___ Beautiful" (Cocker hit): 2 wds.
6 Palm starches
11 100, in Italy
12 "You ___ kidding!"
13 Just not done
14 Came up in conversation
15 Cooking pot
16 Chapeau
17 Under, in poems
19 Certain NCOs
20 "Ol' Rockin' ___" (album by Tennessee Ernie Ford)
21 Products of glaciation
24 Meal for a vulture
26 Trojan hero
27 Jumbles, confusions
30 "Uska Dara" singer Eartha
31 U.N.'s U ___
33 "Raw Like Sushi" singer Cherry
35 "Top ___ mornin' to you": 2 wds.
36 Massey of "Jet Over the Atlantic"
37 Sycophant
38 Hoisting device
39 Beach
40 Lively dances
41 Prides of lions?

Down

1 Moss Hart autobiography: 2 wds.
2 More authentic
3 1915 Claude Debussy work: 4 wds.
4 Brown fur
5 Tic-tac-toe victory
6 Volvo rival
7 Picks up
8 W.W. II Third Army commander: 3 wds.
9 Geneses
10 Some editorial notations
18 Aesop's also-ran
22 Sony rival, initially
23 Bridge seat
25 Insect part
26 "Dinner Rush" star Danny
28 "Where are you?" reply: 2 wds.
29 Lumber measures
30 Dough filled with potatoes
32 Fuss: hyph.
34 Witches, to Shakespeare
37 Mil. award

Across

1 Way to measure pulse rates, initially

4 Alex of "Blazing Saddles"

10 Ducks in ___: 2 wds.

12 "___ Girl" (Trey Songz song): 3 wds.

13 Mitchell mansion

14 Not subject to change

15 Surgical holders

17 Rich in foliage

19 French seasoning

22 Ghost's cry

24 Cousin of rage

25 B-F links

26 Mag. staff

27 Herbert of the "Pink Panther" movies

28 Charlotte of "Bananas"

29 Quilting party

30 Cockney residence

31 Ques. response

32 Slip up

33 Incurred, as debts: 2 wds.

35 Decorative strip

38 Serenaded: 2 wds.

43 New Rochelle, N.Y. college

44 Acts theatrically

45 Lady of Lisbon

46 Off the water

47 ___-Tiki

Down

1 Flying mammals

2 Kind of fall

3 One who doesn't accept defeat easily: 2 wds.

4 1995 No. 1 hit for Seal: 4 wds.

5 Certain colonist

6 Suffix for jambo or kedge

7 Oscar nominee Stephen ___

8 Continue

9 For example

11 Fall off

16 Create clothes

18 Sana'a native

19 Clippings container

20 "Echo Party" rapper

21 Spike and Ang

22 Tony winner Neuwirth

23 German border river

34 eBay competitor

36 ___ account (never): 2 wds.

37 Indian bread

38 Big body of water

39 Morning hrs.

40 Kabuki kin

41 Certain Pontiac letters

42 Artist Gerard ___ Borch

98

Across

1. Dads
6. Bamm-Bamm's foursome
9. Circulatory chamber
11. Apple product
12. Cooking fuel
13. Bag of chips, maybe
14. Bill collector?
15. Hot Wheels toy company
17. Asia's Trans ___ mountains
18. Fortune 500 company based in Moline, Ill.
19. Cut, as a log
20. Desperate: 2 wds.
21. Big pitchers for water
23. Hebrew letters
26. Bavarian river
30. CB, for one
31. Batmobile "garage"
32. Marcos of the Philippines
34. Counterfeiters' nemeses: hyph.
35. Prefix with -phile
36. Damon, to Pythias
38. Agitated state
39. Taoism founder: hyph.
40. Non-Rx, initially
41. ___ more (several): 2 wds.

Down

1. Tortellini, rigatoni, etc.
2. ___ the Hun
3. Like some undergrad studies
4. Bad job for an acrophobe: 2 wds.
5. Closest star to Earth, with "the"
6. Acted badly
7. Capital of Lesotho
8. Drag
10. ___-and-pop store
11. Meeting place
16. It's after Shebat
20. "___ a Liar" (song by the Bee Gees)
22. "___ I Be?" Shrek song
23. Melodic
24. Keen
25. Blissful
27. Reproductive cell
28. "Be that as it may...": 2 wds.
29. Furnish
33. I.W.W. rival
37. P.V. Narasimha ___, 1990s Indian P.M.

99

Across

1 Lichen component
5 Turkish V.I.P.s
9 It may be spared: 2 wds.
12 As expected
13 ___ & the Blowfish (rock band)
14 "Carmen Jones" song: "___ Love"
15 Kindled anew
17 Backstabber
18 Fix, as a fight
20 Harnessed together
22 Battery type: abbr.
24 Retirement community restriction: 2 wds.
27 PC support staffers, for short
29 ___ Tower
30 Muslim form of salutation
32 Get ahold of
33 Others, in Oaxaca
35 Thespian's rep: abbr.
36 Waitress on "Alice"
38 Conversational filler: 2 wds.
40 Lease figure
42 Descend, as from a train
45 Baltic Sea feeder
46 Glossy fabric
47 Outfielder Lee ___ 1959–71
48 Blind segment

Down

1 Part of N.C.A.A.: abbr.
2 Killer of J.F.K.
3 Actor who married Amal Alamuddin in 2014: 2 wds.
4 Commedia dell'___
5 Sum (up)
6 Protector: 2 wds.
7 Ski resort near Snowbird
8 Part of CBS: abbr.
10 Overly smooth
11 Pro Football Hall-of-Famer Sanders
16 Bout enders, in brief
18 Soaks, as flax
19 Police officer training school in Plainfield, initially
21 ___ out (manages)
23 Powwow
25 Downer
26 Rank above senior airman, initially
28 Hindu garment
31 Rock's Michelle and Cass
34 Ward of "CSI: NY"
36 E-mail header
37 Mother of Castor and Pollux
39 Isles
41 Three: It.
43 "Isn't ___ bit like you and me?" (Beatles lyric): 2 wds.
44 Big blast maker letters

100

The grid (crossword puzzle)

Across

1. ____ and seek
5. Murders: sl., 2 wds.
11. "Ain't it the truth!"
12. Ancient ascetic
13. Get rid of pent-up energy: 3 wds.
15. ____ premium: 2 wds.
16. "Love Story" composer Francis
17. ____-Foy, Que.
18. Framework
20. ____ longa, vita brevis
21. 2007 Tao Lin novel "Eeeee ____ Eeee"
22. Two, to Otto
23. Rusty of "Make Room for Daddy"
26. Gets bested
27. ____ end (over): 2 wds.
28. Suffix with cash
29. Slowing, in mus.
30. Judge
34. Tire meas.
35. Robert Burns' "The Bonnie ____ Thing"
36. "____ Ng" (They Might Be Giants song)
37. Bay of Naples attraction: 3 wds.
40. Numbers puzzle
41. Big house in Britain
42. Prickly plant
43. IRS identifiers

Down

1. Label for Arab meat dealers
2. "...____ man with seven wives...": 3 wds.
3. Coup ____
4. "Another Green World" composer
5. Scratch up
6. Actor Davis of "Do the Right Thing"
7. "C'____ la vie!"
8. Goes up and down
9. Hanging out up high, like a bird: 3 wds.
10. Batman, to the Joker
14. Ace
19. Adolescent
22. Japanese thonged sandal
23. One pulling strings?
24. Under debate: 2 wds.
25. "Waltzing ____"
26. Mountain Community of the Tejon Pass, Calif.
28. Angry
30. Began to stir
31. ____ bar
32. "____: The Smartest Guys in the Room" (2006 documentary)
33. Berates
38. Aurora, to the Greeks
39. Mukasey and Ashcroft, for short

Across

1 Suffix for photo

6 Big donors, initially

10 Embarrass

11 Encore telecast

13 "Goodbye, ___ Jean" (opening line of "Candle in the Wind")

14 "What ___" (Mindy McCready song): 3 wds.

15 Antlered animal

16 Brit. news network

18 "Hey, you!"

19 Stocking material

21 Plum's center

22 First main part of the Constitution: 2 wds.

24 Richard of "Chicago"

26 Marlin or Cardinal, e.g.

27 Lively Spanish dance for two

29 "Big Blue"

30 Imitator

34 Gun enthusiasts' org.

35 Dungeons & Dragons game co., initially

36 Over or on: prefix

37 U.S.-born Japanese

39 "The Seven Year Itch" actor Tom

41 Like "20 Questions" answers: 2 wds.

42 French toast

43 Like Jack Sprat's diet

44 Move with a splashing sound

Down

1 Swindler, slangily

2 Carlo Levi's "Christ Stopped at ___"

3 DEA figures: var.

4 Doctrine

5 Process in which the product of one thing is the stimulus of the next: 2 wds.

6 Gutenberg's invention: 2 wds.

7 J.J. Pershing's command in W.W. I

8 Undermine

9 More foamy

12 Nights, in Napoli

17 New Year, in Hanoi

20 Solid

23 Fill to excess

24 Archangel who appeared to Zacharias

25 In one group: 2 wds.

27 Like a fish

28 Forbiddances

31 Green half of the band Gnarls Barkley?

32 Impressive mark: 2 wds.

33 Prepared surface soil

38 Alfonso XIII's queen

40 ___-Mart (retail chain)

102

Across

1 Goes back, like the tide
5 Homeopathy predisposition
10 Bearded animal
11 Hanna-Barbera cartoon character: hyph.
12 Capital of Norway
13 Eager
14 "The Paris of the Orient"
16 Shepherd's locale
17 Eat or drink quickly or greedily, slangily
21 Great quantity
23 Casa dweller
24 "The Rumble in the Jungle" victor
25 Leaves in a cup
26 "Holy cow!"
29 Externalize, in a way
31 Defeat soundly, in slang
32 PC linkup
33 Picnic sporting event: 2 wds.
37 Strip of meat in a Tex-Mex treat
40 Spin like ___: 2 wds.
41 Charm
42 Be slack-jawed
43 Certain recesses
44 Ultimatum ender

Down

1 Driving forces
2 "Poppycock!"
3 Russian guitar
4 Removed the pits from
5 Bog
6 Mild antiseptic
7 "How to Succeed in Business Without Really Trying" librettist Burrows
8 Ham, to Noah
9 Witticism
11 Companion of "humbug"
15 Auto-tank filler
18 Before birth
19 Some bucks
20 Brotherhood, for short
21 "___ who?"
22 Cut short
27 Store, as corn
28 Pair seen in winter
29 Animal found in Finland
30 Car house
34 Alley animal
35 Officers
36 Fencing sword
37 Airline overseer, initially
38 Fuse abbreviation
39 Au ___ (served in its own gravy)

Across

1 Geisha's girder
4 Draper of "Mad Men"
7 Pen
9 Golf score
12 Clad
13 ____ Victor
14 20–20, e.g.
15 Shipping hazard, briefly
16 Ad headline
18 Showy flowers
20 Be indisposed
21 Playing marble
22 Poetic palindrome
23 "Honor ____ father"
24 Apprehend
27 Coagulates
29 Make a knot
30 Prearranged situations: hyph.
32 "There is nothing like a ____"
33 Central point
34 Tugboat sound
36 Ortiz, Hilda of 'Ugly Betty'
37 Kind of law
40 "The Fresh Prince of ____-Air"
41 Toward the land: 2 wds.
42 Toil and trouble
43 Angler's catcher

Down

1 Wood sorrel
2 Computerized task performer
3 Highbrow type
4 ____ straits (serious trouble)
5 Short-term affair: hyph., 2 wds.
6 Aussie outlaw Kelly
8 Number of digits on one hand
9 Demonstration
10 A lot of lot
11 Riches preceder, sometimes
15 Small amount
16 Freelancer's enc.
17 Epitome of lightness
19 Sunbeams
21 Above
25 Ability to hit a target
26 Buzzer
28 Neighbor of Ger.
30 Strikebreaker
31 Fish-eating eagle
32 "The lady ____ protest too much"
35 Estimator's phrase: 2 wds.
37 Extinct flightless bird
38 "____ you for real?"
39 Release, with "out"

104

Across

1 "Spider-Man" costar Willem

6 Elephant Boy of a 1930s film

10 "Stop, sailor!"

11 Place for a pin

12 Arrogant talk

14 Cable choice, initially

15 At high volume

16 Follower of an Eastern philosophy

18 Amaze

21 Doesn't go crazy: 2 wds.

23 Indian bread

25 Sch. groups

26 Stewed meat in a thick white sauce

30 One of the Seven Dwarfs

31 For the full length of a pregnancy: 2 wds.

33 Speak noisily

34 Footnote abbr.

36 Mutually destructive

40 Martini's partner

41 Aunt in Toulouse

42 Jai ___ (fast-moving sport)

43 Fencing swords

Down

1 A bit loopy

2 ___-garde

3 Better than good

4 Org. founded by George Soros in 1993, initially

5 Series ender: 2 wds.

6 Beach grains

7 Shrinks' org.

8 Sleeping spot

9 Suffix with nod or caps

11 Ill-mannered types

13 Having a red hue

17 Concerning the ear

18 Level reached by the sea

19 ___ dare: 2 wds.

20 Anderson or Craven

22 Admiral Graf ___

23 TV's "Mayberry ___"

24 "___ y Plata" (Montana's motto)

27 Computer company

28 Scattered

29 Tampa neighbor, briefly: 2 wds.

32 Betting game

33 "___ am" (answer to "No you're not"): 2 wds.

35 Broccoli hearts?

36 Money for old age, shortly

37 Khmer Republic leader

38 Aviation counterterrorism agency, initially

39 Hat

105

Across

1 Brick type
6 Mantric mutterings
9 Astronomer's sighting
11 Los Angeles street gang member
12 ___ table (dines): 2 wds.
13 Beauvais's department
14 Trendy berry
15 Crazy Horse, e.g.
17 Check
18 Sub finder
19 Composer of "Rule, Britannia"
20 Raids
21 Horton the Elephant creator
23 Certain fir
26 Some community bldgs.
30 Apple desktops
31 Sally in "Boston Legal"
32 As yet: 2 wds.
34 "___ Peach" (The Allman Brothers Band album): 2 wds.
35 "The Ghost and Mrs. ___"
36 Clear
38 "Girl With ___ Hat" (Vermeer): 2 wds.
39 Soccer score, sometimes: hyph.
40 Extra notes at the end of a letter, initially
41 Sol, e.g.: 2 wds.

Down

1 Cochise portrayer of 1950s TV, Michael ___
2 Frost remover: hyph.
3 Acquire
4 It has one's name and company information: 2 wds.
5 Italian note
6 Writer Fallaci
7 Lose
8 Catches, in a way
10 From ___ Z: 2 wds.
11 Ideas for interior decoration: 2 wds.
16 Mil. aides
20 Giant syllable
22 Atlantic Coast states, with "the"
23 JPEG alternative
24 Parisian passions
25 Women
27 It's "short and stout" in a children's song
28 Focal point
29 Gardener, at times
33 "Evil Woman" grp.
37 Verb suffix

106

Across

1. Cynic's scoff: 2 wds.
5. 1450, in Rome
9. Siberian port city
11. After, in Avignon
13. Religious building
14. Fire up
15. Govt. agency once headed by Steve Preston
16. Plow furrow
18. Org. for Heat, Hornets and Hawks
19. Stain removal product, initially
20. "Good ____ Been to You" (Dylan album): 2 wds.
21. ____ Nidre (Day of Atonement prayer)
22. Old magazine billed as "America's Aviation Weekly"
24. Apprehensive
26. International ____ (diplomat's area)
28. Lodge
30. Attire
33. Hospital sections, initially
34. Mets and Marlins div.
36. "____ wise guy, eh?": 2 wds.
37. "Forrest Gump" setting, familiarly
38. Baseball great Young et al.
39. R.V. hookup provider
40. "SNL" alum Cheri
42. Hand part
44. Kidney enzyme
45. "Kiss the Spider Woman" actress Braga
46. For men only
47. Furniture chain

Down

1. Lake ____, source of the Mississippi
2. Mishandle (a ball)
3. Shame felt when a guilt is made public
4. Literary inits.
5. Simone ____, Italian painter of "The Anunciation" (1333)
6. 1970s sitcom "____ Sharkey"
7. Completely wasted: 4 wds.
8. Sappho's home
10. Actress Sedgwick
12. Simmons rival
17. As a rule
23. Frequently, in poetry
25. Part of a joule
27. Sport using the foil, épée, and sabre
28. Pay tribute to
29. Gives a speech
31. College pal
32. "____ Black Sheep" (kids' rhyme): 2 wds.
35. Ballpark figs.
41. Creek
43. ____ polloi (common people)

107

Across

1 Fills out
6 Hole that an anchor rope passes through
11 Dismay
12 "___ not amused!": 2 wds.
13 Payment alternative to checks: 2 wds.
15 Part of Q & A, briefly
16 Goes off, in a way
17 ___ Fjord
18 He had the first billion-view YouTube video
21 Throw in, as a question
23 Racer Ricky
25 Guitarist Phil
26 Where goods are displayed
30 Reaction to Niagara Falls, often
31 ___ of Spain, Trinidad
32 "___ Colors" (Cyndi Lauper chart-topper)
33 Pro-Bowl defensive end Umenyiora
36 "Spin City" actor: 3 wds.
40 C.S. Lewis' lion
41 "Ditto!": 3 wds.
42 Mockery, of a sort
43 Prefix meaning "nine" that can precede -gram

Down

1 Ole Miss rival
2 ___ reflection
3 Hospital carers, initially
4 Actor Hakeem ___-Kazim, Colonel Iké Dubaku in "24"
5 Least ingenuous
6 Intense shock
7 "No ifs, ___ ..."
8 Little, in Scotland
9 "Certainly, ___!"
10 Letter before "tee"
14 Heraldic border
17 French wave
18 Rhymer's writing
19 Draft org.
20 "Uh-huh"
21 Doing nothing
22 Connive
23 Pretoria's country letters
24 Dennis Williams' org.
27 Jumped (out)
28 Don Juan, e.g.
29 End of a threat: 2 wds.
32 Word after "greater" or "lesser"
33 In the blink ___ eye: 2 wds.
34 "___ Like It Hot"
35 Ornamental plant
36 Calf's cry
37 Initially, you'll need one to get online
38 151, to Nero
39 ___ Stewart, former host of "The Daily Show"

108

Across

1 Pat
4 Limit
7 Courtroom figs.
10 Nest egg money, at first
11 Brit. award letters
12 Singleton
13 Mentalist's forte: hyph.
16 In a fitting way
17 Some garden workers
20 ____ out (managing)
24 "Life is not ____, it is a gift": 2 wds.
25 Break down
26 Former Serbian capital
27 Cause of inflation?
28 "Age of Unreason" series author Gregory
31 Saab competitor
33 Bluish gray
34 City on the Rhone
35 Boxing site
37 Spread far and wide
43 That, in Toledo
44 Louse-to-be
45 Dietary oil source
46 Supply with staff
47 Suffix with arch or art
48 U.S. flag color

Down

1 Slow-witted
2 Onassis nickname
3 Prohibition
4 Body
5 Aid an arsonist, say
6 Rang out
7 "What ____ care?": 2 wds.
8 TV journalist Curry
9 Part of a line: abbr.
14 Jeanne ____, French heroine
15 Dick Van ____ of "Mary Poppins"
17 "Forest Gump" actor Tom
18 Architectural projection
19 Cushy school course: 2 wds.
21 "____ Your Name" (Beatles song): 2 wds.
22 Gullible
23 Spinning toys
29 Followers of zetas
30 Pacific
31 "____ Fair" (Thackeray novel)
32 "The Plague" setting
36 Arab chieftain
37 Clinton, e.g.: abbr.
38 "The Heart ____ Lonely Hunter": 2 wds.
39 Royal wish
40 Horizontally: abbr.
41 Pedicure target
42 TV announcer Hall

109

Across

1. D.J.'s stack
4. Canonized Mlle.
7. Outside: prefix
10. Mouths, zoologically
11. Battery buys, initially
12. Measure of conductance
13. Killjoy, slangily: 2 wds.
16. Duck, in German
17. More likely
18. Caprine animals
21. Head of France?
22. "Peter Pan" role
24. Scrubbing brand
25. "___ in Seattle" (1993 romcom starring Tom Hanks)
28. "Hath ___ sister?" (Shakespeare): 2 wds.
29. Carpentry need
30. Consumes
32. Character in Byron's "Don Juan"
35. Modify
37. "Dumb" girl of old comics
39. Purpose of existence: 2 wds.
42. Bottom-of-letter abbr.
43. Game pieces
44. Driveway stuff
45. 95 or 66: abbr.
46. Turkish honorific
47. "It's ___-win situation": 2 wds.

Down

1. Handle adversity
2. Sturm's companion
3. Painter Andrea del ___
4. For instance
5. Listening device
6. Those, in Spain
7. Queen Victoria, for one
8. Frito-Lay snacks
9. Strait between the Coral Sea and Arafura Sea
14. Bait
15. Away from the office
19. Counterfeiter catchers: hyph.
20. Floral leaf
23. Author Wiesel
25. Material used to make something airtight
26. Framework
27. Leave out
28. Listener
31. French pronoun
33. "Whole ___ Shakin' Goin' On"
34. Firth of Clyde island
36. Massenet opera
38. Dynamic start?
40. Not positive: abbr.
41. Paternity identifier, initially

110

Across

1 Medieval war clubs
6 Arguments
11 "The Gift of the Magi" device
12 Army attack helicopter
13 Capital of Tanzania: 3 wds.
15 "The ___ Daba Honeymoon"
16 Folk song "Jolly Roving ___"
17 Have a bit of, as brandy
18 "Well, ___ be a monkey's uncle!"
19 Taconite, e.g.
20 Addition
21 Spring (from)
23 "___ quam videri" (North Carolina's motto)
24 Freetown currency unit
26 "Yo!" alternative
29 Gusto
33 Short sleep phenomenon?
34 1-1 game, say
35 "The Matrix" character
36 Victorian, for one
37 Big roll, as of cash
38 ___ cross
39 Garden center purchases
42 Pennies, sometimes
43 Present
44 Plagued, as by problems
45 Teens who wear black makeup, e.g.

Down

1 Above ground level
2 Fit for farming
3 Reef components
4 Chemical suffix
5 Part of a heartbeat
6 Alarm
7 Sen. or Rep.
8 Loses prestige
9 Park features
10 Taste
14 Relating to tailoring
22 Last, for short
23 1997 Koji Yakusho film, with "The"
25 Short of
26 Factory-made, as housing
27 Calm
28 Common sense
30 Absorbed
31 "___ me!"
32 Colonials and split-levels, e.g.
34 Chubby Checker's dance
40 Pipe joint
41 Lion's home, maybe

111

Across

1 Kind of dance

4 The Knicks, the Celtics, et al.

7 Some radios, initially

10 P.V. Narasimha ___, 1990s Indian P.M.

11 Mouths, anatomically

12 Head slapper's cry

13 Natives of Canberra, e.g.

15 Al Jolson's real first name

16 Model Banks

17 From the U.S.: abbr.

18 Sensitive to criticism: hyph.

21 Hyundai or Honda

22 Fortune 500 inits.

23 Held accountable

28 Soak, old-style

29 559, to a Roman

30 Chinese dim sum dish: 2 wds.

34 Pastoral expanses

35 Feed bag contents

36 Suffix with Salvador

37 Kitchen set

40 "___ tu" (aria for Renato)

41 Clandestine maritime org.

42 Suffix with north, south, east or west

43 The Sunflower State: abbr.

44 ___ crossroads: 2 wds.

45 Calendar abbr.

Down

1 Singsong syllable

2 Nonprofessional sports grp.

3 Office message notes: hyph.

4 Some roulette bets

5 Moment at which something gives way: 2 wds.

6 "___ in apple": 2 wds.

7 Rhett's last words: 2 wds.

8 The Louvre, par exemple

9 Pottery fragment

14 Brief summary

17 Cure for what ails you

18 Pitch

19 Clamor

20 "___ up to you"

24 Dutch "uncle"

25 Used dynamite

26 French flower

27 Business card no.

30 Built for speed

31 "I ___ Symphony" (hit for The Supremes): 2 wds.

32 Took to jail: 2 wds.

33 Actress Raymonde, Alex Rousseau on "Lost"

37 ___ good turn: 2 wds.

38 Certain numero

39 Abbr. in a business letter

112

Across

1 "Concentration" puzzle
6 Word meaning determiner, usually
11 Nitrogen compound
12 Amalgamated
13 In good working order
15 Office computer system
16 Diminish
17 One pill, maybe
20 "C'est la ___!"
22 Tokyo, once
23 Blasted
27 Reflection: 2 wds.
29 "ER" extras
30 Brothers and sisters, e.g.
31 Casual attire
32 Abstain from food
33 Does a hit man's job
36 Light source
38 Frank
43 1,000 kilograms
44 "Gladiator" setting
45 Hard work
46 Good to have around

Down

1 Brit. bombers
2 Australian bird
3 Coal carrier
4 "I give up!"
5 ___ good example: 2 wds.
6 Spaceship, maybe
7 Shaft of light
8 Katmandu's continent
9 Fellow, for short
10 Add a fringe to
14 Scottish city
17 Moore of "G.I. Jane"
18 Chief Norse god
19 Separate by color, say
21 "Under the Net" author Murdoch
23 Hardly the life of the party
24 "We'll ___ kindness yet, for auld lang syne..." (Robert Burns): 2 wds.
25 Auspices
26 Mar, in a way
28 Greek wine
32 "La Traviata" mezzo
33 Chooses, with "for"
34 Course
35 Church, poetically
37 Brightly colored food fish
39 Ball stopper, sometimes
40 "Mad Men" account executive Cosgrove
41 "Parade's ___" (Ford Madox Ford tetralogy)
42 "I'm against the motion"

116

113

Across

1 "Midnight Cowboy" character Rizzo's nickname
6 Wound the pride of
11 Russian tennis player Vesnina
12 Fool, slangily
13 Guys
14 From the East
15 Scott Turow novel: 2 wds.
16 Barre room bend
17 Flash of light
19 Thing settled in a bar
22 College V.I.P.
24 "Wheel of Fortune" request: 2 wds.
25 Hard-rock center: 2 wds.
26 Small fry
28 Ancient Egyptian priest
29 Back talk
30 Waste
32 Start of a Chinese game
33 Composer and diarist Ned
34 Raised mark on the skin
36 Clothing
39 Cover story
41 Bad treatment
42 Turkish money
43 Perry ____, Earle Stanley Gardner's detective
44 Coeur d'____, Idaho
45 Salad ingredient

Down

1 San ____, Italy
2 Country singer Jackson
3 Message carrier, once: 2 wds.
4 Fishhook attachments
5 Mex. and Uru. are in it
6 Biblical poem
7 "You're looking at him," formally: 2 wds.
8 Practically silent: 4 wds.
9 Put ____ fight: 2 wds.
10 Early night, in an ode
16 Handheld source of shade
18 Snack, say
20 Rare blood type: abbr., 2 wds.
21 "I've Gotta ____" (Broadway musical song): 2 wds.
22 Soothing ointment
23 I.C.A. predecessor
27 ____ Bingle (Crosby moniker)
31 Home mixologist's spot: 2 wds.
33 Poker ploy
35 Meir contemporary
37 Mil. aides
38 Chamber workers: abbr.
39 Part of the Deep South: abbr., 2 wds.
40 Diamond gal of Broadway
41 Matador producer, initially

114

Across

1 Al Capone henchman Frank
6 Encouraged, with "on"
11 Lake Geneva spa
12 Eddy who made money in the 1950s and 1960s
13 Johnston McCulley literary creation
14 Not too hot, like a burner: 2 wds.
15 Sufficient, informally
17 Women, to a buckaroo
18 Bassist Claypool
20 Avatar of Vishnu
22 Acknowledge
24 Calm
28 Player
30 Best Actor of 1958
31 "Just a mo!": 2 wds.
33 "Revenge" getter of film
34 Heavy, durable furniture wood
36 Phone six letters
37 Architect Mies van der ____
40 ____ double take (looked again): 2 wds.
42 "What now?!"
44 Pamplona runners
47 Actress Oberon
48 Attempts
49 Class that doesn't require much studying: 2 wds.
50 "Golden ____" (David Bowie song)

Down

1 ____ Percé
2 Literature Nobelist Andric
3 Dreadfully dull
4 Glacier-formed lake
5 "Peace ____ time"
6 Tokyo, formerly
7 Kipling classic
8 Inaugural ball, e.g.
9 Carbon compound
10 Moistens, in a way
16 Mis followers
18 Titicaca, por ejemplo
19 "____ Almighty" (2007 film)
21 Checkers, e.g.
23 Like some winds
25 Rosary recital: 2 wds.
26 Seabird that can be "sooty"
27 Prefix meaning "within"
29 Riddle-me-____
32 Blackguard
35 Baby cat
37 "Ben Hur" setting
38 Roman "olive"
39 ____ de combat
41 Scale start: 2 wds.
43 Crime-busters' grp.
45 Done, to Donne
46 Barbecue sound

115

Across

1 Infected with bacteria
7 Agronomy concern
11 Italian cheese
12 Round buyer's phrase: 2 wds.
13 Ted of "Cheers" and "Curb Your Enthusiasm"
14 ___ cava
15 Abolishes: 3 wds.
17 Napkin holder
19 Yorkshire river
20 Letters in a classified ad. indicating a willingness to negotiate
21 Antares and Betelgeuse, e.g.: 2 wds.
25 Sea eagle
26 Some ranges, initially
27 Wallace of "E.T."
28 1963 Jack Kerouac novel: 2 wds.
30 Greetings
31 Nativity figures
33 Ethyl finish
34 Hardening of body tissue
38 Action at the office
39 Ready to be engaged: 2 wds.
42 Book after Proverbs: abbr.
43 Redecorate: 2 wds.
44 Encrusted
45 Florida beach town, familiarly: 2 wds.

Down

1 Low
2 What that is in Spain
3 Indoor ball game: hyph.
4 Zap with a stun gun
5 Patsy Cline's "___ Pieces": 3 wds.
6 Food, clothing, etc., intended for direct use: 2 wds.
7 Cold War adjective
8 Lacking height or depth: hyph.
9 "___ Angel" (Mae West comedy): 2 wds.
10 Book part
16 Automatic updates from favorite websites, initially
17 Classical Library founder
18 Rock shelter at the base of a cliff
22 Glue, e.g.
23 Bit attachment
24 Mobutu ___ Seko
26 Gum used as a thickening agent
29 Rotten
32 Argumentative retort: 2 wds.
34 Design criterion, briefly
35 ___-Cola
36 Key's partner
37 Breakfast chain acronym
40 Not working any more: abbr.
41 Before, to a sonneteer

116

Across

1. Decorative loop
6. "I haven't got it ___!": 2 wds.
10. Big name in astrology
11. Poet's "below"
13. Argentine dance
14. Organ-playing singer from Kaka'ako: 2 wds.
15. Tour organizer, for short
16. Start of the day
18. Danger in Afghanistan, initially
19. Round vegetable
20. Brief leaf?
21. Bettered "Better Homes and Gardens," say
23. Chest muscles, for short
24. I.R.S. employee: abbr.
25. Flier to Copenhagen, initially
26. Feudal underling
28. Bank info: abbr., 2 wds.
31. "Be on the lookout" message, initially
32. Letter from St. Paul: abbr.
33. Kind of battery, initially
34. Archaic term for one's father's mother
36. Black-throated ___ (Asian bird)
37. Clear
38. Handy
40. Bacteria discovered by Theodor Escherich: 2 wds.
41. Sunday singers
42. Massachusetts motto opener
43. Smallville family

Down

1. Baked entree: 2 wds.
2. Envisioned
3. Breakfast buffet choice: 2 wds.
4. Alternative to net
5. Walked heavily
6. Hindu god of war
7. Broadway brightener
8. Appearance in bodily form, as of a ghost
9. Italian, e.g.
12. Cletus and Boss of "The Dukes of Hazzard"
17. Ref. staple
22. Calendar abbr.
23. D.C. fundraiser
25. Fool, casually
26. American symbol
27. Make neat, smart, or trim
28. Shrinks' org.
29. Ace a test: 2 wds.
30. Horse operas
32. "Frasier" dog
35. Lagerlöf's "The Wonderful Adventures of ___"
39. Most common English word

117

Across

1. Mideast native
6. "___ sow, so shall…": 2 wds.
10. Ancient: hyph.
12. Code in which many Web pages are written, initially
13. Spicy condiment
14. Circus crowd's sounds
15. "Don't get any funny ___!"
17. Scottish "no"
18. Crash site?
20. Rodrigo Díaz de Vivar: 2 wds.
22. Certain plaintiff, at law
24. Like tears
27. Flip-flop
29. Phone corporation (1984–97)
30. Spanish sirs
32. Earthy prefix
33. "Maria ___" (Jimmy Dorsey #1 hit)
35. Mount Olympus dweller
36. Infomercials, e.g.
38. Well-known knife brand
40. Brainy sort
42. Soap ingredient
45. Fit
46. 1924 gold medal swimmer
47. Comic book dog barks
48. Back, in a way

Down

1. Adage
2. Turkish for "lord"
3. Irrational (with worry, grief, etc.): 2 wds.
4. Course
5. "A Delicate Balance" playwright
6. "Bingo!"
7. Acting as a sentinel: 2 wds.
8. Jewish youth org.
9. "Anything ___?"
11. Disappearing phone features
16. Digitize a picture
18. Calls' partner
19. "A Hard Road to Glory" author Arthur
21. ___ Ulyanov, Vladimir Lenin's father
23. Chem. ending
25. Famous fiddler
26. Biblical bk.
28. Kinnear of "The Kennedys"
31. Long-billed wading bird
34. It's marked by a "-" on a battery
36. Eastern pooh-bah
37. "___ me!"
39. "Nana" star Anna
41. "Star Trek: Voyager" character
43. ___ Poke (caramel sucker)
44. Cut, as a tree

118

Across

1 Indian nursemaid
5 Mirror ___
10 Archeological find
12 Afflictions
13 "Farewell, mon ami"
14 "Reversal of Fortune" star
15 Oversized
16 Flower-shaped decoration
18 Third generation Japanese-American
20 Egg layer
21 Like Death's horse, in Revelations
23 Org. until 1993
24 Raised mark on the skin
27 Country great Haggard
29 Paddle's cousin
30 Part of a leaf, perhaps
32 Female gametes
33 Classic theater name
37 Abandons
40 Hemingway book "The Old Man and the ___"
41 Purple shade
42 Bake, as eggs
44 Correspond, in grammar
45 Alpine air?
46 Extremely: 2 wds.
47 "Bill & ___ Excellent Adventure"

Down

1 Keffiyeh wearers
2 News shows, newspapers, etc.
3 Adjust, in a way
4 Make haste
5 Nile bird
6 Filly's mother
7 Repeat order at the bar
8 Refined
9 Gist
11 Solution to any problem: hyph.
17 "Texas tea"
19 Day ___ (place for a pedicure)
22 Diplomatic mission
24 Tree feller
25 Try it out: 3 wds.
26 Operation with a pencil
28 Sushi ingredient, often
31 Reject, with "out of"
34 "All kidding ___..."
35 Waxed, old style
36 Counts, now
38 All square
39 Thatch bit, perhaps
43 Sweltering

119

Across

1 Canadian peninsula
6 Ligneous fiber
10 Peacemaker Sadat
11 Multiple-choice letters: 4 wds.
13 Volleyballer/model Gabrielle
14 Words on a Renault 5: 2 wds.
15 Iowa State University's town
16 Eyeball layer
17 It may be picked
18 Small batteries' letters
19 Function
20 City west of Beijing
22 General Robt.: 2 wds.
23 Newspaper chiefs
25 ____ Club (Costco rival)
27 Occupying a taxi: 3 wds.
30 Young dog
31 Songwriters' grp.
32 Wall St. debut
33 Outfit for baby
35 Seized vehicle, briefly
36 Others, in Madrid
37 Wrinkled
38 Stay put, nautically: 2 wds.
39 Spoken
40 "Beauty and the Beat" rapper
41 Rhone tributary

Down

1 M1 rifle inventor John
2 Sickle-cell ____
3 Not easily irritated: hyph.
4 Big donors, initially
5 Before, to Blake
6 Makes a bundle
7 Aid a criminal
8 Economics or politics, e.g.: 2 wds.
9 Hypnotic state
12 Box
16 E. L. Doctorow novel
18 Kind of cuckoo
21 Takes too much, for short
22 Jazz or Beat
24 Military intelligence agency, initially
25 Ribbon holder
26 Em, to Dorothy
28 Enter the picture
29 Money gained illegally, slangily
31 Another name for the buffalo
34 ____ spell (rested briefly): 2 wds.
35 "Recipe Rehab" host Evette
37 56, in old Rome

120

Across

1. "All hat ___ cattle" (pretentious): 2 wds.
6. File coating
11. Fashionable mushroom
12. Dogpatch denizen Hawkins
13. Enjoys the pool
14. Part of the leg
15. Like Alberta's tar sands: hyph.
17. Dive (for)
18. Amount owing
20. Grass grown for hay: hyph.
25. Eskimo boat
27. "A Confederacy of Dunces" author
28. Expenditure
30. Pleased as punch
31. Oscar winner Mercedes for "The Fisher King"
33. Harvey Bullock of "Gotham": 2 wds.
38. "Wheel of Fortune" host Pat
39. Comic strip about a girl in high school
40. Popular aquatic performer
41. ___ Martin (Bond film car)
42. Architect Saarinen
43. ___ way out (finds a solution): 2 wds.

Down

1. "I ___ over this…": 2 wds.
2. "___ get it": 2 wds.
3. What a chuck holds: 2 wds.
4. Sedative drug
5. Ashley of "Full House"
6. ___ Band, Bruce Springsteen's primary backers: 2 wds.
7. When doubled, a food fish
8. ___ chief (mag. boss): 2 wds.
9. Actress Diana
10. "Uh-huh"
16. A U.S. Dept.
18. Bill and Hillary Clinton, e.g.
19. Flightless ranch bird
21. Kennel
22. Barrier where people must pay to go further
23. Commercial suffix with Rock
24. Sidewalk denizen, informally
26. Asian sheep breed
29. Deborah's "The King and I" costar
32. Fitzgerald and others
33. Author Roald
34. California resort city
35. It might be dropped
36. Ones in Spain
37. Danish opera composer, August (1859–1939)
38. Flagstaff to Tucson dir.

121

Across

1 Eastern titles
5 R.N. workplaces
9 Laser printer powder
11 Artificial waterway
13 Relative value
14 Magistrate in ancient Rome
15 Like some vbs.
16 Film buff's channel, initially
18 "That's ___ funny"
19 Rudyard Kipling snake
20 Scooby-___ (dog detective)
21 Little kid
22 European erupter
24 Mary-Kate and Ashley
26 Substitute: hyph.
28 Whine
30 ___ A Sketch (red toy)
33 Subordinate employee
34 Cleared (of)
36 Debtor's letters
37 "We ___ the World"
38 Suffix with cap or coy
39 Bit of resistance
40 Extra benefit
42 Sleep trouble
44 Terrific, in Hollywoodese
45 Get wiser
46 Jazzman Saunders
47 Jubilant delight

Down

1 Hit forcibly
2 Warn (someone), as a lion might: 2 wds.
3 Unwillingness to change one's views
4 Six, to Italians
5 Freezing: hyph.
6 No-goodnik
7 Not meant
8 Oater bar
10 Part of a Hope-Crosby film title
12 Baltic natives
17 Like a romantic evening, maybe
23 Four-wheeler, initially
25 German pronoun
27 Deodorant type
28 Unions don't like them
29 "You can't squeeze in": 2 wds.
31 Be united
32 Compassionate
35 Do business (with)
41 Former U.S.S.R. member
43 Game piece

122

Across

1 Early pulpit
5 Mob bosses
10 Curb, with "in"
11 Large meteor that explodes
12 "Cogito, ___ sum"
13 Eye problem
14 Bird's beak
15 Lingered over lunch, e.g.
16 Bed
17 Gasteyer of "Saturday Night Live"
18 One of the primary colors
19 Cast
20 Shakespearean verse
22 Midterm, e.g.
23 Enterprise, energy and initiative: hyph.
25 Source of "It is more blessed to give than to receive"
27 Good for consumption
30 "Am I an idiot!"
31 Append
32 Word with "foreign" or "first"
33 Calif. neighbor
34 Accept
35 ___ lepton (physics particle)
36 Restaurant tables
38 Auditory
39 Implant deeply
40 End of a terse challenge
41 Leo of "You Make Me Feel Like Dancing"
42 Bassoon, e.g.

Down

1 Bowls
2 Fine wool
3 Origin possibility: 3 wds.
4 "Bottoms" filmmaker Yoko
5 Removed the center of
6 "Heroes" star Larter
7 Fierce fight in close combat: 2 wds.
8 Abhorrent
9 Group of six
11 Die, slangily: 3 wds.
15 Square footage
21 Denials
22 Clavell's "___-Pan"
24 Go around and around, in a way
25 Building blocks
26 Eclipse phenomenon
28 Be a go-between
29 Brought out
31 Dislike, and then some
37 "Little piggy," really
38 "___ the fields ..."

123

Across

1 Neckerchief
6 Navigational aid
11 Speciality
12 Make mushy
13 Woodwind instrument
14 Quartz variety
15 Rotten to the core
17 Passing notice
18 Hi-____ (like some graphics)
19 Little seal
21 State of anger
22 Barrel bottom bit
24 World Cup sport
26 Illustration explanation
28 Fear
30 Town, so to speak
33 Cyclotron particle
34 ____-tac-toe
36 Impair
37 "Goodbye Columbus" author Philip
39 Nine-day Catholic prayer
41 Fourth month
43 Becomes more lively (with "up")
44 Copy exactly
45 Omani money
46 W.W. II conference site
47 Part of a tennis court

Down

1 Be able to spare
2 Join two pieces of metal
3 Common auto feature: 2 wds.
4 Bus driver on "The Simpsons"
5 Get ready to drive: 2 wds.
6 Tax preparer, for short
7 Science fiction's ____ Award
8 Any of 0, 1, 2, 3, etc.: 2 wds.
9 Stop working
10 Move unsteadily
16 Provide with nourishment
20 Taro dish
23 Blarney-stone kisser's gift
25 Part of an ear
27 Peach center
28 Hijacking
29 Major publicity
31 Stick in one's craw
32 Covered with turf
35 Coconut flesh
38 Help for a solver
40 Obscure
42 Meadow

124

Across

1 Create

6 Some Italian cars, for short

11 "Peace ____ time": 2 wds.

12 and 31 Down "227" sitcom star

13 Erstwhile detergent brand

14 In any way: 2 wds.

15 Thor Heyerdahl craft: 2 wds.

16 Bedwear, briefly

18 Kennedy Library architect

19 Paper fasteners

21 Part of a balance

22 Use a needle and thread

23 Partner, old-style

24 Lacking flavor

27 .45 maker

28 Clover site

29 Certain Internet feed

30 Substance that blinds temporarily: 2 wds.

34 Private address, initially

35 Sitcom planet

36 "May ____ excused, please?": 2 wds.

37 Ends of fishhooks

39 Color of honey

41 Astronomer Tycho

42 Movie star Clark

43 Rumormonger

44 Someone ____ (not mine)

Down

1 Whirring sounds

2 Member of an Eastern church

3 Ancient Greek colony

4 Light units: abbr.

5 Minute amount of liquid

6 Build a fortune

7 Calif. newspaper

8 Drinks served with crushed ice

9 Very attentive: 2 wds.

10 Briny

17 Diamond seller

20 Furtive summons

23 North Carolina's Cape ____

24 Left over: 2 wds.

25 He almost won: hyph.

26 Accidental escape of a fluid

27 Bad-tempered

30 Out of port: 2 wds.

31 See 12 Across

32 White poplar

33 Withers

38 Antioxidant additive, initially

40 ____ de mer

125

Across

1 Marathon

5 Lemon ____

9 Junípero who founded Franciscan missions in California

10 Sirs' counterparts

12 "What an improvement!": 2 wds.

14 Longboat propeller

15 Ingrid's "Anastasia" costar

16 Laundry detergent brand

17 Alley org.

18 Olive ____

19 Lily in Lille

20 "Lord of the Rings" actor Sean

22 Pastoral poem

24 "____ Secret" Kylie Minogue song: 2 wds.

25 Ho Chi ____ City (former name for Saigon)

27 Excited to the point of disorientation

31 Family head

32 Suffix with appoint or assign

34 Browning's "before"

35 Response: abbr.

36 Metric system prefix

37 Own, to a Scot

38 Newspaper Clark Kent works at: 2 wds.

41 Actor Murphy of "Trading Places"

42 Perfect or past, e.g.

43 Six, in San Jose

44 "Beat it!"

Down

1 Detox centers, briefly

2 Biblical mountain

3 PC component

4 Pleasant to look at: 4 wds.

5 Preparation of ammonium carbonate and lavender: 2 wds.

6 Cheerios grain

7 Not long ago

8 Food Network chef

9 "It's hard to ____ Trane": 2 wds.

11 Married ladies of Spain: abbr.

13 Accept

21 "Am ____ trouble?": 2 wds.

23 "____ Hear a Waltz?" (Broadway musical): 2 wds.

25 Single-celled organisms

26 Private

28 "Star Trek" counselor Troi

29 Most free from moisture

30 Buttinsky

31 Miami-____, southeasternmost county on the U.S. mainland

33 Milk-carton abbreviation

39 52, in old Rome

40 N.R.C. predecessor

126

Across

1 New Test. book
4 Varieties: abbr.
7 Party planner, for short?
10 "What ___ going to do?": 2 wds.
11 Polish off, like pancakes
12 "E-Bow the Letter" band
13 Unblemished find for a book collector: 2 wds.
16 Name derived from the name of a person
17 Former New York Mets manager: 2 wds.
22 Horace, for one
23 Start of a French oath
24 "___ Can Cook"
25 Place of learning in Albuquerque, initially
26 Last in a series
29 Folk rocker ___ Curtis
31 Song from "The Little Mermaid": 3 wds.
33 "La Loge" artist
34 Sandwich bread choices: 2 wds.
39 Off-road goer, for short
40 Early role-playing game co., initially
41 Driving force
42 Ed.'s request
43 Lean-___ (camping structures)
44 Flushed

Down

1 Son of Noah
2 One of the big four record labels once, initially
3 Coal holder
4 Don't stop: 2 wds.
5 Carpentry grooves
6 Smarts
7 Butcher's best: 2 wds.
8 Fair-hiring agcy.
9 K-O connection
14 Bus. card data
15 Banks on the runway
17 "___ Believe?" 2015 movie starring Mira Sorvino: 2 wds.
18 Give ___ (care): 2 wds.
19 Hard hit baseball: 2 wds.
20 "Sesame Street" regular
21 Greek valley where games were held
27 Thousands, slangily
28 Newsman Peter
29 Cricket sounds
30 Prefix with nautical
32 Bit of statuary
34 ___ in king (spelling aid): 2 wds.
35 ___ loss: 2 wds.
36 Celtic sea god
37 Shirt size: abbr.
38 Put down new lawn

127

Across

1 Boom box abbr.
4 Barcelona bear
7 Sarah Palin, e.g.
9 Baltic or Bering
12 Like a gridiron
13 "Fantastic Mr. Fox" director Anderson
14 "Damages" actor Donovan
15 High-priority
17 More sore
19 Zap
20 "Idylls of the King" character
21 "Joy of Cooking" instruction
22 700 to Nero
24 "China Beach" setting, in short
26 Wanna-___ (poseurs)
27 Morlock morsels in "The Time Machine"
29 Korea Bay feeder
31 Butts
32 Caught
35 Breakfast cereal
37 French girl, briefly
38 Tally (up)
39 Hardest on the eyes
41 "Law," in Spanish
42 Destroy
43 "Quietly Brilliant" phone company letters
44 Orlando to Miami dir.

Down

1 Gozo Island is part of it
2 ___ artery
3 "Cut the jokes!": 3 wds.
4 River to the Volga
5 "___ at the movies": 2 wds.
6 Dilly
8 Greet and seat: 2 wds.
9 Drip with fear: 2 wds.
10 Minuscule: var.
11 Common flowers
16 Fast sports cars, for short
18 "... ___ Berliner"
22 Skin-related
23 Composer Debussy
25 Baby goat sound
28 Magazine: abbr.
30 55 miles an hour, maybe
33 "Someone ___ America" (1996 film)
34 Raison ___
36 Elbow-bender
40 Anita Brookner's "Hotel du ___"

128

Across

1. Edward James of "Miami Vice"
6. Iron, e.g.
11. Warm dry mountain wind: var.
12. Bouquet ____
13. 1970 James Taylor hit: 3 wds.
15. Prefix with -syncratic
16. Scottish golfer Sandy
17. City southeast of Tel Aviv
19. "Avatar" costar Stephen
21. Clapton who sang "Layla"
23. Playwright Norman
27. Hive horde
29. Diarist Samuel
30. Spanish sirs
32. Casual agreements
33. Submachine gun
35. Deighton of thrillers
36. Bombers' or fighters' locations, initially
39. Small stream
41. Soviet economic policy
45. "Adios": 2 wds.
46. ____ vincit amor
47. Opera singer Simon ____
48. "Popeye" creator

Down

1. Not at work
2. Law, in Limoges
3. Circle of longitude
4. Expressed surprise
5. Very slow creature
6. Letters on some beer bottles
7. Tea flavored with bergamot: 2 wds.
8. Cafeteria holder
9. Shade of blue
10. Long, narrow mark or band
14. "Language and Mind" author Chomsky
17. Not as much
18. "… ____ should grow too fond of it": R. E. Lee: 2 wds.
20. Forty winks
22. Type of squint: hyph.
24. Naming the letters of a word
25. Overstated praise
26. Pt. of PGA
28. "The A-Team" actor: 2 wds.
31. Noted Spanish muralist
34. Bananarama's "Robert de ____ Waiting"
36. Altar area
37. Professional charges
38. ____ Harte, U.S. writer
40. Capital of Togo
42. Carrier to Oslo, shortly
43. Rio and Sedona maker
44. River to the Rhine

129

Across

1 Roadside sign
4 Author Lewis et al., initially
7 Tree juice
10 Award bestowed by Queen Eliz.
11 Ear-related prefix
12 Six-pointers, for short
13 Wick holder: 2 wds.
15 "___ for Iceberg": 2 wds.
16 Feline with a Magic Bag: 3 wds.
18 Shoe specification
19 Publicity, casually
20 Glows
22 Birdlike
25 Aircraft accident investigators, initially
26 Greek 'Gray Sister' who shared an eye and a tooth with Deino and Pemphredo
27 Island in the Aegean
29 Anxiety
30 "Mogambo" first name
31 Dizzy's genre
32 Eternally
37 Comic strip cry
38 Shoreline problem
39 "Evita" role
40 "Cry ___ River": 2 wds.
41 "The Sound of Music" extra
42 Kid
43 School grouping in some states, initially
44 Gunpowder or Earl Grey

Down

1 Amusing act
2 "___ Baby" (song from "Hair")
3 Economic situation in which goods are scarce: 2 wds.
4 Cajoles
5 Mo.-end document
6 Actress Loren
7 Obstacle to progress: 2 wds.
8 Sarah McLachlan hit of 1998 (or, backwards, an opera)
9 "Hey you!"
14 Rest on top of: 2 wds.
17 Makes poisonous
20 Part of Q & A, briefly
21 "Respect for Acting" author Hagen
23 Sailors' assents: var.
24 Pessimist's word
28 Queen song: 2 wds.
29 Overseas
32 Indisputable item
33 Eight, in Spain
34 "___ Tú" (Mocedades hit)
35 Don Juan, e.g.
36 Central Sicilian province

130

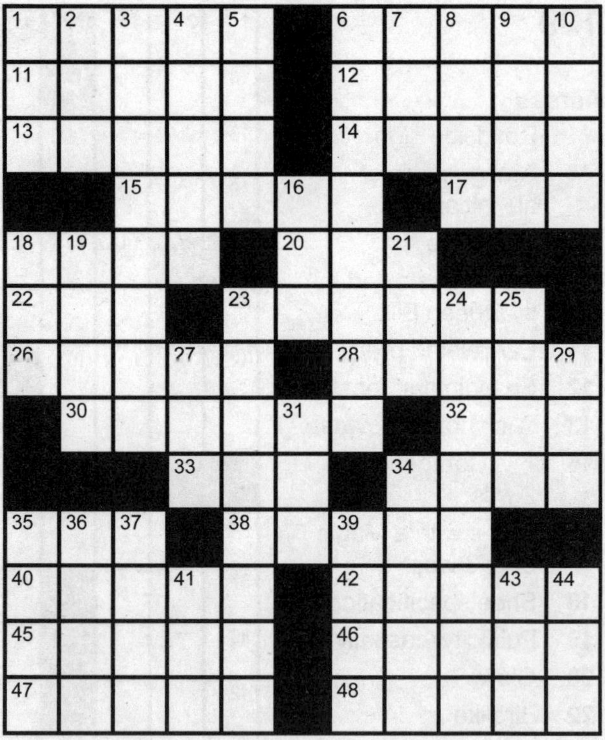

The grid (crossword puzzle) with numbered cells.

Across

1 Houses, in Spain
6 Italian form of bowls: var.
11 Harebrained
12 Depth charge target: hyph.
13 "Children of a Lesser God" director Haines
14 "Personal Best" director Robert
15 Palindromic belief
17 Gibbon species
18 Arthur and others
20 Elementary school class
22 Glamorous Gardner
23 Cain/Law movie of 2007
26 John ___ Garner, one-time vice-president
28 Enjoy to the fullest
30 Dog
32 Prompt an actor
33 Little troublemaker
34 Foal's mother
35 Welsh mountain valley
38 Former NFL player in Calif.: 2 wds.
40 Give a grand speech
42 Early year: 2 wds.
45 Caleb and John Dickson, for two
46 ___ Haute, Indiana
47 "All Quiet on the Western Front" star Lew
48 Have a try: give ___: 3 wds.

Down

1 Geom. figure
2 Gasteyer formerly of "SNL"
3 City in western El Salvador: 2 wds.
4 South American high points
5 Talk show host Hannity
6 Projecting support for a wall
7 Letters indicating price flexibility
8 Hood
9 Jesus's water-into-wine city
10 Ancient road to Rome
16 One-time domestic flight co.
18 Forbid
19 "Well, Did You ___!" (Porter classic)
21 River that flows through Mirandela, Portugal
23 Like some stockings
24 What news anchors face, briefly: 2 wds.
25 60 minutes
27 ___ de coeur
29 Suffix for chicka or campo
31 Facial business
34 Painter of "The Spanish Singer"
35 ___-Cola
36 "King Kong" star Fay
37 1965 PGA champ Dave
39 French roast
41 Roman trio
43 Notable W.W. II neutral: abbr.
44 ___ gratias

131

Across

1. Shot, for short
5. Compliment
9. ___ Tower
11. Claim as one's own, as land
13. Pelvic bones
14. "The Italian Job" actor Michael
15. ___ Grove Village, Ill.
16. Gangster's gun, for short
18. 252 wine gallons
19. Bow
20. Before, in poems
21. Native of Benin, Nigeria
22. "Buona ___" (Italian greeting)
24. Depress
26. Level
28. "The ___ of Swat"
30. Ailurophobe's fear
33. "48 ___" (Eddie Murphy movie)
34. Lobster eater's garb, for some reason
36. Definite article word
37. "Go team!"
38. Cold cubes
39. Anger
40. Not fitting
42. Single-master
44. Anatomical sac
45. Metric weight
46. "Laugh-In" segment
47. "Previously owned," in ad-speak

Down

1. Ledger column
2. South African maize plant
3. Porbeagle: 2 wds.
4. "Bobby Hockey"
5. Milky
6. Alicia of "Falcon Crest"
7. Organization of countries set up in 1945: 2 wds.
8. Strip away, as a forest
10. Astute
12. Air component
17. Element #33
23. Behave
25. Elmer, to Bugs
27. Home
28. Poison oak, e.g.
29. Distant planet
31. Seat of power
32. Oozed
35. #1
41. Telekinesis, e.g.
43. "Skip to My ___"

132

Across

1. Fond du ____, Wisconsin
4. Day ____
7. ____ water (it's from the faucet)
10. Adaptable
12. In the style of: 2 wds.
13. Jack, author of "On the Road"
14. ____-sequitur
15. Highest rank or level: hyph.
17. Express a point of view
19. Test, as ore
20. "Where the Wild Things ____"
21. Do poorly
22. Plant of the borage family: hyph.
28. Versailles to Paris dir.
29. Astonish
30. Lee or Levi's, for jeans
33. Photographer's request
35. Musical theme
37. The NHL's Senators, on scoreboards
38. Reflexive pronoun
41. Sea monster
42. Beat it
43. "Shoulda thought of that"
44. ____ Avivans (some Israelis)
45. "I approve"

Down

1. Albanian currency
2. Drink in a mug
3. Famed French jewelry company
4. Bonehead
5. "La Vie en Rose" singer
6. Enthusiastic approval
7. Flavors
8. Hello, in Waikiki
9. Undergarment
11. Any minute now
16. "Cast Away" setting
17. Blockhead
18. Ace
21. Gobbled up
23. Fellow, for short
24. Last in a series
25. Innocence: var.
26. Bird that's a pet for Harry Potter
27. Football kicking tool
30. Bank deposit?
31. Backward-looking, in fashion
32. Common aspiration
33. Baseball datum
34. "Gorillas in the ____"
36. First word of "The Raven"
39. Civil War general
40. Rx org.

Across

1 Put into words
4 "Come at me, ___" ("Jersey Shore" tag line)
7 Dirty digs
10 It's cold, regardless of climate
11 Church title, for short
12 It's Japanese for "carp"
13 Compensation
16 In a cool manner
17 Protection in a secure place
23 Music Appreciation, for one
24 Exodus commemoration
25 "American Gladiators" co-host Laila
26 Bitter feeling
27 Connections
30 Heat source
32 Expected hopefully
34 Contents of some cartridges
35 Noisy quarrel
41 Round, green vegetable
42 Blackguard
43 "___, four, six, eight, who do we appreciate?"
44 Element in a "Wizard of Oz" character's name
45 Brief time periods
46 Undertake, with "out"

Down

1 "Dear" one
2 Trick taker, often
3 "Amen!"
4 Building blocks
5 Adjust, as laces
6 Small eggs
7 Compete in the Winter Olympics, maybe
8 "___ bad!"
9 Yang's counterpart, to the Chinese
14 Associations
15 Label A or B, e.g.
17 La ___
18 Beat: 2 wds.
19 Get the vapors and fall down
20 Dostoyevsky novel, with "The"
21 Audacity
22 Midas's undoing
28 Charlie Brown had trouble flying one
29 Burn
30 Catches, in a way
31 Bakery buy
33 Rack up, as debt
35 Quick, as a pupil
36 "Fantasy Island" neckwear
37 "Baywatch" complexion
38 Of a thing
39 "I ___ you one"
40 "___ a chance"

134

Across

1 ____ Sorvino, Amy Whelan of "Intruders"
5 Diminish
10 Aces, sometimes
11 Feline crossbreed
12 Sticky fragrant resin of the terebinth tree
14 Pension supplement, for short
15 Concede
16 North African fox
18 Greek and Roman, e.g.
21 Alliance
23 U.N. agcy. concerned with working conditions
24 Brute follower
27 Polynesian rain dances
29 "Die Meistersinger" heroine
30 Ivan the Terrible, for one
32 Goes off course
34 Baroque
38 Gave out
40 Rossini's "La Donna ____ Lago"
41 Item seen in court?: 2 wds.
43 Alleviated
44 Appropriately named fruit
45 Hammock cords
46 Bungle, with "up"

Down

1 Recurring theme
2 Accustom
3 Aired again
4 Death on the Nile cause, perhaps
5 Magnet alloy (trade name)
6 Angler's hope
7 Good at gymnastics, maybe
8 Ivy feature
9 Bard's "before"
13 Hole in your shoe
17 "30 Rock" network
19 C.S.A. state
20 "Rescue me!" letters
22 Sailor's maps
24 Tina of "30 Rock"
25 Egg cells
26 Injustice: 2 wds.
28 Big container
31 Stripes' counterparts, in pool
33 Hearing, taste or touch
35 "Time is money," e.g.
36 Leaks
37 Island in New York Bay
39 For the second time, say
41 Magnum, for one, slangily
42 Work shirker

135

Across

1 Done
6 Break off
11 "You've ____ Friend to Me" (Bryan Adams song)
12 Country of the U.K.
13 Liquid flowing through the body
15 "Rock and Roll, Hoochie ____" (1970s hit)
16 "Majesté" preceder
17 One-time bathroom brand, ____-Flush
20 American capital, initially
22 ____ nutshell: 2 wds.
23 Place to put the feet up
27 Be off-target: 3 wds.
29 Move like a snake
30 Gerund's end
31 New Deal prog.
32 Oozy horror film menace
33 "The West Wing" actor
36 "____-Devil"
38 Done with care and thoroughness
43 ____ Boingo, "Weird Science" band
44 Rushed, as to attack: 2 wds.
45 Words to live by
46 "Jack Sprat could ____ fat ...": 2 wds.

Down

1 Recede, as a tide
2 Classical pianist Anton
3 ____ volente
4 Mushroom used in Japanese cooking
5 Pedestal part
6 100 lbs.
7 Noble's domain
8 Out of the wind
9 They can get choppy
10 Salinger heroine
14 Compass point at 135 degrees
17 "The ____" (life simulation game series)
18 Indigo dye source
19 ____ goreng, Indonesian fried rice
21 Ending for gang or poll
23 Will-____-wisp: 2 wds.
24 It's in the bag
25 River that flows through Pisa
26 1940s Soviet state security org.
28 Weird
32 Fertile valley of east Lebanon
33 Part of the Bible: abbr.
34 Grizzly's hangout
35 Sup
37 Fabled racer
39 Landscaping stuff
40 Bank acct. entry
41 One of the Bobbsey Twins
42 Classic muscle car initials

136

Across

1 Switches

6 "Desire Under the ___"

10 It used to be Pleasant Island

11 Change, chemically

13 Actor, singer, dancer, e.g.

15 Pilot's announcement letters

16 ___ Alamos, N.M.

17 African antelope

18 Go one of two opposite directions

19 "___ what?!"

20 "Do the Right Thing" director

21 Biblical paradise

23 Ashes, e.g.

25 Bloodless

27 Desserts, to many dieters

29 Roll-top, for one

33 ___ Remo, Italy

34 Finish, with "up"

36 "___-Pan" (James Clavell novel)

37 Mission control, for short

38 Dash lengths

39 Attila the ___

40 Right of the accused: 2 wds.

43 Even if, briefly

44 Neighborhood

45 ___ Mix

46 Like a teen's room, stereotypically

Down

1 Allergic reaction

2 Classified: hyph.

3 Power ___

4 Grand ___ ("Evangeline" setting)

5 Bad-tempered

6 Kind of mark

7 Hawaiian wreath

8 Fabric press

9 Movie parts

12 "___ Grit" (1969 John Wayne film)

14 Delicious

22 Masefield play "The Tragedy of ___"

24 Beatles tune, with "The"

26 By hook or by crook

27 Flamethrower fuel

28 Like some inspections: hyph.

30 High standards

31 Hot spots

32 Royal

33 Living room piece

35 Biblical poem

41 Density symbol

42 Sushi topping, sometimes

137

Across

1   Cat's place for petting
4   Good club?
7   Barker or Marley
10 Big shooter
11 Dance for one person: 2 wds.
13 Consider carefully
15 Hokkaido native
16 New Mexico's state flower
17 Sacred beetle of ancient Egypt
20 ____ Heyerdahl
21 Very dry, as wine
23 River to the North Sea
24 Part of the US–Mexico border: 2 wds.
27 P.I.
28 Gumbo thickener
29 Bread maker
31 Charge
35 Happen again
37 Fluish feeling
38 Likelihood
41 Heavy, waterproofed cotton cloth
42 Get prone
43 One-seventh of the rainbow
44 None has two
45 Boundary

Down

1   "Star Wars" director George
2   Before the appearance of life (geology)
3   Feather, zoologically
4   Animal that beats its chest
5   Video recorder, for short
6   Sports achievement award, initially
7   Stranded out of the water
8   Result
9   Makes dim, old-style
12 Hussy
14 ____ charger (engine performance enhancer)
18 Ben Affleck movie of 2012
19 Muslim woman's garment: var.
22 Cutting
24 Daydream
25 Chilled: hyph.
26 Port city in northeastern Brazil
27 Lethargy
30 Small protuberances
32 Nimble
33 Interrupt a conversation: 2 wds.
34 Atwitter, with "up"
36 Croupier's tool
39 Container
40 Plug-____ (computer patches)

138

Across

1. Glory
6. Loses hair
11. In reserve
12. In progress
13. Principle
14. Backgammon piece
15. Excitement
16. Gamble
18. ____ talk
19. More sophisticated
22. Groom-to-be
24. Peanut and sesame
28. Fool, slangily
29. Latest craze
30. "The Last of the Mohicans" girl
31. Punched
32. Roof of the mouth
34. Celestial body
37. Clear the tables
38. Canadian comedienne Luba
41. Spread out
43. Combine
45. USMC member
46. To any degree: 2 wds.
47. Some parties
48. Haul heavily: var.

Down

1. Karate exercise
2. Employed
3. Reptile of the Mesozoic era
4. Shelley work
5. Check in progress
6. Prepare a roast
7. Fore partner
8. Ankh feature
9. Finished
10. Dance lesson
17. Apple picker
20. Open, in a way
21. Celeb's playful ribbing
22. License giver, initially
23. U.N. workers' grp.
25. Built-in
26. Engage in mendacity
27. Lamentable
29. Poisonous fumes
31. Bird ____
33. Deep fissure
34. "Lord of the Rings" baddies
35. Origin
36. Afghanistan region, Tora ____
39. Look up and down
40. Cry of pain
42. Gas-guzzling stat.
44. Ending of the Bible

139

Across

1 Rest day: abbr.
4 Set (against)
7 Add years to one's life
8 Plaster finishes
13 Levelheaded: 3 wds.
15 Musical composition
16 Alway's antonym
17 Chitchat
18 Port town on the coast of the Sea of Japan
19 Revised before printing
22 Russian fighter plane
23 Become less intense: 2 wds.
25 Prevent
27 It recounts Dido's suicide
29 General talk, hearsay
31 Matter in the Big Bang theory
33 Sch. whose song is "The Eyes of Texas"
34 Saffron-flavored dish made of rice with shellfish
36 Jay Leno rival: 2 wds.
38 Artsy one
39 Not, to a Scot
40 GBP alternative
41 Mdse.

Down

1 1978 Peace Nobelist
2 Ancient meeting places
3 Perplexity
4 Attention-getters
5 "Was ___ harsh?": 2 wds.
6 Mon. follower
9 "This ___ be!"
10 Sandwich cookie center: 2 wds.
11 "SNL" alumna Cheri
12 "Who knows?" gesture
14 Cell phone company
18 Eat to excess, shortly: 2 wds.
20 Rimsky-Korsakov's "The Tale of ___ Saltan"
21 A foot wide?
24 More magical or elflike
25 ___ Banner, secret identity of the Hulk
26 Cars
28 Remove element 82 from
30 Brilliantly colored fish
32 Long tresses
34 ___ and pans
35 Out for the night
37 Modern: Ger.

140

Across

1 Pop's kin
4 Dance bit
7 "___ Kapital" (Karl Marx)
10 ___ ammoniac
11 Augmented fourth in music
13 Scented sheet used in a storage area: 2 wds.
15 Daughter of King David
16 "Endymion" poet
17 German drinking salutation
19 AT&T competitor
21 Sachet holding leaves for infusion: 2 wds.
25 Up to me: 3 wds.
28 Whiskey made from potatoes
29 First president of South Vietnam, ___ Dinh Diem
30 The ___ State (Connecticut nickname)
33 Sketch comedy series inspired by a magazine: 2 wds.
36 Scale
39 Country entertainment: 2 wds.
41 Actor Kurt
42 Band associated with Elvis Presley
43 Water___ (flosser)
44 Cpl.'s superior
45 The ___ Glove (hot surface mitt)

Down

1 DOT, alternatively
2 Japanese capital (710–84)
3 "Beverly Hillbillies" name
4 Wing (prefix)
5 Abbr. on some sheet music
6 More smooth
7 Spanish lady
8 Without ___ (dangerously): 2 wds.
9 Sun. talks?
12 Cravat pin: var.
14 Armed conflict
18 Daring film feat
19 Econ. measure
20 ___ many irons in the fire
22 Meet head on: 2 wds.
23 H.S. class
24 Shine, in ad-speak
26 Gossips at the synagogue?
27 Outputs of artists
31 Onetime Golden Arches' offering
32 Highest note in Guido's scale
33 Fig. on a car sticker
34 Here, in Spain
35 Time of long shadows
37 1205, to Romans
38 Lilith's portrayer on "Cheers"
40 Finnish-American actress and dancer Taina

141

The grid (blank crossword):

Across

1. Attended: 2 wds.
6. Karmann-___ (sports car)
10. Old Oldsmobile
11. Make a dash toward: 2 wds.
13. Measuring instrument that uses echoes
14. Chief Vedic god
15. Medical care grp.
16. Ways to go: abbr.
18. Starter: abbr.
19. Inconceivable stretch
20. Frozen "wasser"
21. Tape format, initially
22. Nabokov heroine and others
24. Japanese golfer Isao ___
26. "The Wreck of the Mary ___"
28. King with a golden touch
31. Classic theater name
33. Cousin's mother
34. "Either you do it, ___ will!": 2 wds.
36. Where cops work, initially
38. Made a meal of
39. Candy that has its own dispenser
40. ___ rule: 2 wds.
41. Law, in Lyon
42. Float ___ (arrange financing): 2 wds.
44. R. D. ___, "The Divided Self" author
46. "Peanuts" boy with a blanket
47. Credence Clearwater Revival song "___-Q"
48. "Let them eat ___" (Marie Antoinette)
49. Trailing

Down

1. Explosive part of a missile
2. In the latest fashion: 3 wds.
3. Resort city south of the Grand Canyon: 2 wds.
4. Parseghian of Notre Dame
5. Yankee leader Joe
6. Astronaut Gus
7. Attila the ___
8. Make personal
9. Cry of frustration
12. Catches some rays
17. Day: Sp.
23. Letters of success, initially
25. Korean car maker
27. Stretch
29. Willa Cather heroine
30. Actor Rod or composer Rand
32. Gridiron gains: abbr.
34. Fire ___ (gem)
35. Archeologist's find
37. Latin dance
43. Arctic diving bird
45. Gold: prefix

142

Across

1 "Big ____" (Notorious B.I.G. hit)
6 Son of Jacob and Zilpah
11 "The Little Mermaid" mermaid
12 Fifth wheel
13 Embroidery on canvas
15 Carbonated quaff
16 Hidden
17 Distort
19 Bar
22 Approached the bench?
25 Reform-minded
28 Congressional measure
29 Couch
30 Harness racer
32 "____ Street" (famous kids' show)
35 Europe's most active volcano
39 Dread, misgiving
41 Buenos ____
42 All-too-public tiff
43 Chicago's NFL team
44 Chronic nag

Down

1 Balance parts
2 ____ balls (chocolate covered treats)
3 ____ Piper
4 Educator
5 "Is that ____?"
6 In accordance with: 2 wds.
7 Go bad
8 Hearty hello
9 Coastal flyer
10 Given up working: abbr.
14 Disappeared gradually
18 Oslo's country: abbr.
19 Feature of a nice hotel
20 Leap across a gap, electrically
21 "Thanks a ____!"
22 Be in session
23 Many a D.C. road
24 Ball raiser
26 "It's right over there!"
27 Duration
30 "____ or plastic?"
31 Awry
32 "I'll take a ____ at it"
33 Northernmost Pennsylvania county
34 It comes twice after "Que" in a song
36 Layer, as of a wedding cake
37 "With malice toward ____ ..." (Lincoln)
38 "I Found ____ Baby": 2 wds.
40 Onager, e.g.

143

Across

1. Buffaloed: 3 wds.
8. Nut
9. Get down on one's knees
12. Relating to the sole of the foot
13. "Earth Girls ___ Easy" (Julie Brown song)
14. Big success
15. Long vowel mark
17. Greenfly, e.g.
20. Analyze, in a way
21. Fatty secretion
23. Flower fanciers
24. Barely enough
26. Health resorts
28. Blood bank patron
30. Eminent
32. Exposed
34. Come to light
36. African antelope
37. Casbah headgear
38. Composer Aaron
41. Finish, with "up"
42. Property recipient, at law
43. Migratory grasshoppers

Down

1. First letter, to Greeks
2. Dutch export
3. Curse or declare to be evil
4. PC linkup
5. Giant slugger Mel
6. "The King and I" locale
7. Tiny bit, as of food
9. Calliope cousins: 2 wds.
10. Jagged, as a leaf's edge
11. Inheritance, of a sort
16. Beach shelter
18. Wading birds
19. Dark horse
22. Central, in combinations
25. Protesters, sometimes
26. Big mess, slangily
27. Skin openings
29. Milk curdler
31. Sticker on a windshield
33. Bros
35. ___ contendere (court plea)
39. Snapshot, for short
40. Money in Moldova

144

Across

1 Q trailers
4 Varnish ingredient
7 V-mail address, for short
8 Berlin wail
9 They put out blazes: abbr.
12 Brand with a spinnaker logo
14 Actor Stephen of "V for Vendetta"
15 Bk. of the Bible
16 Get the customer to spend more
18 Chef Lagasse who says "Pork fat rules!"
20 "My So-Called Life" actor Jared
21 Political cartoonist called "our best recruiting sergeant" by Lincoln
22 Muezzin's call to prayer
23 Certain noblewoman
26 "Dedicated to the ___ Love" (hit for The Mamas & the Papas): 2 wds.
27 No longer working: abbr.
28 "___ la Douce" (1963 film)
29 Short synopsis
32 Filbert
34 "Saving Private ___"
35 Suffix with arbor or app
36 European language

38 1950s political monogram
39 Punched-in-the-gut grunt
40 Class-conscious org.?
41 "Weekend Update" show, initially
42 Prime meridian std.

Down

1 Hindu queen: var.
2 Burst
3 French for "all together": 2 wds.
4 My ___, Vietnam
5 Adoption of customs, beliefs, etc.
6 Crack, in a way
9 Preserving by cooling rapidly: hyph.
10 Some river mouths
11 Beauty parlors
13 Spartacus, e.g.
17 Slovenly woman
19 Prefix with thermal
23 Expressed in speech
24 Bit of progress
25 Fiber knot
30 Checks out
31 Flip one's lid?
33 Roswell sightings: inits.
37 Patriot's org.

145

Across

1 Auctioneer's responsibility, essentially

5 Ancient Greek coin

9 Medicinal plants

11 ___ Circus (old Vatican area)

13 Former 20-dollar coin: 2 wds.

15 Concealed

16 They're filled at the pharmacy, for short

17 "When We Were Kings" subject

18 Bring to bear

19 Attend as an observer: 3 wds.

21 Belgrade native

23 Latin American shawl: var.

24 Turf intro

26 Win over

29 Popular college guy, initially

33 "Siddhartha" author Hesse

35 One type of nest egg, briefly

36 Land in la mer

37 Company with a dog in its logo, initially

38 Popular wine, for short

39 Not large or small: hyph.

42 Fluid transition

43 Gland: prefix

44 Inf. unit

45 Foreword: abbr.

Down

1 Hindu holy men

2 Horror movie directed by Robert Legato

3 With more volume

4 Independent nat. since November 1941

5 Poor movie rating: 2 wds.

6 "___ sport": 2 wds.

7 Princess Leia ___

8 Move in an ungainly way

10 Some cameras, initially

12 Angler's gear

14 Being

20 Ethnic group of Ethiopia

22 Emerald City's creator

25 Red shade

26 Wedges

27 More slippery

28 Bring (up)

30 One of a ship's main masts

31 Get situated

32 Openness

34 "Apollo 13" org.

40 Grooved on

41 Former dictator ___ Amin

146

Across

1 Calendar days, briefly
5 In sufficient quantity
10 Sections
12 Blender button
13 Roughly
14 Friend, to Francisco
15 Holy title: abbr.
16 "30 Rock" network
18 Nuoc ___ (Vietnamese fish sauce)
19 Former partner of Lennon
20 Homer Simpson shout
21 Visited a restaurant, with "out"
22 Short pencil
24 Synapse neighbor
26 Hit the spot
28 Gist
30 Edible roots
33 Thickness
34 Hawaiian dish
36 Barn bird
37 Lawyer's thing
38 A hallucinogen, initially
39 Ballad
40 Really outlandish
42 Call forth
44 Milk accompaniment
45 Cão da Serra de ___ (dog breed)
46 Breaks in
47 First word of "Send In the Clowns"

Down

1 Typist's shortcuts
2 "Murder on the ___ Express"
3 Body network sending signals: 2 wds.
4 Midwest Indian
5 Geronimo's people
6 Buttoned up
7 Red, green, and blue, e.g.: 2 wds.
8 Musically connected
9 Royal protectors
11 Hourglass fill
17 Relatives of tunas
23 "Humph!"
25 Amateur video subject, maybe
27 Like open convertibles
28 Displace
29 Membrane enveloping a lung
31 Come to
32 Least ingenuous
35 Concept
41 Future fry
43 Seven, to Caesar or Nero

150

147

Across

1 Pieces of money
6 Long tale
10 Listlessness
11 Cyclist
12 Concerning punishment
13 Moderate
14 Hard to solve, complex
16 Big oil cartel, initially
18 Dazzling effects
22 World's swiftest mammal
24 Futon kin
25 Not bottom
26 Sport ____ (all-purpose vehicle)
27 Top vineyard
28 Enjoyed a buffet
29 Hoodwink
31 The back, in medical textbooks
33 Far from ruddy
34 Stitched folds
36 India's first P.M.
39 Sovereign time period
42 Sign of the zodiac
43 Run away to get married
44 Pyramid's bottom
45 Church assembly

Down

1 Porcini mushroom
2 A wee hour
3 Hostelry owner
4 Subtlety
5 Grain storage building
6 Delphic figure
7 Letters before a crook's name
8 Grasp
9 Bruno Mars song "Just the Way You ____"
11 Quantities of goods produced at one time
15 British ritual
16 Group of eight
17 Snap
19 Attainment of a position of power
20 Religious scroll
21 Detailed analysis
23 Burial mound
30 Of recent times
32 Consumer's binge
35 Aphrodite's lover
36 Pick up
37 Golden ____ (great time)
38 U2 "If God Will Send ____ Angels"
40 U.S. document publisher
41 Nancy Drew's boyfriend

148

Across

1 100 cents in South Africa

5 Drawn forcibly, historically

10 "The Tourist" author Steinhauer

11 Roman memory goddess

12 One way to reduce a sentence: 2 wds.

14 Group of schools in one area, for short

15 Antipollution org.

16 Outdoor sports store

17 Ornamental hangings behind an altar

19 Compass dir.

20 A quarter of four

21 ____ Ration, dog food brand: hyph.

22 "The Plague" author Albert

25 Shipping weights

26 Crooked

27 "Cry ____ River": 2 wds.

28 ____ juris (of age)

29 Choral composition

33 Weather org.

34 "____ Enterprise"

35 Baseball great Young et al.

36 Die, slangily: 3 wds.

39 Blood problem

40 Buck or wall addition

41 Health, in France

42 Ala. neighbor

Down

1 Enticed, with "in"

2 Wu-Tang Clan song: "Can It Be ____ Simple": 2 wds.

3 Has got to have

4 Kind of testing, for short

5 Israeli dances

6 "Brokeback Mountain" director Lee

7 Trainee

8 Saint-____ (Loire's capital)

9 Boone and Day-Lewis

11 Sweet flavor

13 Has-____ (over-the-hillers)

18 Early course

21 Southpaw Enterprises, Inc. founder Jim

22 Crenshaw relatives

23 Main constituent of corundum

24 Make damp

25 On edge

27 One of Chekhov's "Three Sisters"

29 Adorable one

30 "Found ____" (song by Ultra Naté): 2 wds.

31 Loser to Lewis

32 ____ Martin (Bond film car)

37 Ambulance worker, for short

38 Not dis!

149

Across

1 Award for winning
6 Be bright
11 Resembling two peas in a pod
12 Praline morsel
13 Part of a cassette tape: 2 wds.
14 Oven emanation
15 Distance indicator
17 Part of a play: 2 wds.
18 Bullfight cheers
21 Kidnaper's demand
25 Sue Grafton's debut mystery novel "____ for Alibi": 2 wds.
26 Not any, in Normandy
27 Metric meas.
28 Like most peanuts
30 New England state, shortly
31 Colorado county
33 Portable guns: 2 wds.
37 Make sure of: 2 wds.
38 Laughter sounds: hyph.
40 Architectural borders
41 Unescorted
42 Strikes out
43 Assail

Down

1 Bell and Barker
2 Exodus campsite
3 "Reverie" singer Benami
4 Cub Scout leaders, in the U.K.
5 Mountain Community of the Tejon Pass, Calif.
6 Like some relationships
7 Analgesic drug
8 Computer image
9 John or Jane, e.g.
10 Old Spanish queen
16 Baked dessert
18 Western treaty grp.
19 "Dark Skate" series artist Halloran
20 Immigrant's course, for short
22 Reggae relative
23 Old-school tough guys, in rap songs
24 Ed.'s submissions
26 Figure on a tax return: 2 wds.
29 Precisely: 3 wds.
30 Team spirit
32 She hid the spies at Jericho
33 Dried
34 Cartoonist Lazarus
35 Electrical units now called siemens
36 Of sound mind
37 Lawn layer
39 Established

150

Across

1 ____ Stanley Gardner
5 Hidden
11 "Breakfast at Tiffany's" actress Patricia
12 Daniel Webster, for one
13 Somerset Maugham novel: 3 wds.
15 Put up, like a building
16 English test item
17 Payment for a road
19 Piece of photographic equipment
22 Actor Nicolas
26 Computer monitor animation: 2 wds.
28 Handel opera, "____ and Galatea"
29 Make fun of
30 Flat-bottomed boat
31 Youth International Party co-founder Hoffman
35 Motown's original name
39 Group action
41 Attraction
42 Opera by Umberto Giordano: 2 wds.
43 Like lowercase i's and j's
44 Speaker's place

Down

1 Ending with defer or refer
2 Rise up on the hind legs
3 Michigan or Ontario
4 Successful candidates
5 Mauna ____
6 Synthetic fiber
7 Little ones
8 Greek Hs
9 "The Big Easy": abbr., 2 wds.
10 Deuce beater, barely
14 Squirrel away
18 10th century pope
19 Civil War inits.
20 Notre Dame's conf.
21 Hosp. procedure
22 Column carved in the shape of a person
23 Prefix with fauna or form
24 H.S. proficiency exam
25 Before, to bards
27 Major mattress maker
30 John of tractors
31 Part of U.S.N.A.: abbr.
32 Long sweeping uppercut in boxing
33 Cloth measure
34 "Why do ____ up with it?": 2 wds.
36 Actress Kunis of "Black Swan"
37 Actress Singer of "Footloose"
38 Hydrocarbon suffixes
40 Communist

151

The grid:

```
 1  2  3     4  5  6
 7           8        9  10 11
12           13    14
15     16          17
18              19
20           21 22    23
       24          25
26 27        28          29 30
31     32          33
34           35 36
37           38       39
40           41       42
             43       44
```

Across

1. N.Y. or Rio, e.g.: abbr.
4. Liq. measures
7. Dockworker's org.
8. Island SSW of Naxos
9. "Pipe down!"
12. Civil War fighter, for short
13. Windpipe
15. Arriving after curfew: 2 wds.
17. Wintry
18. Lone Star State sch.
19. Utah's Senator Hatch
20. Condition of disease
23. Crib sheet user
24. Male graduate
26. Canadian TV channel, initially
28. Dried grapes
31. Country once called Dahomey
33. Look like a wolf
34. Barbara of "I Dream of Jeannie"
35. One of Santa's reindeer
37. Physician who performs operations
39. Hebrew letter
40. Four song releases, typically: inits.
41. Duvet spot
42. Ending for Japan or Sudan
43. Kind of humor
44. Alcoholic's affliction, for short

Down

1. Brightest star in the sky, in Canis Major
2. More than enough
3. Behavior required when eating: 2 wds.
4. Brad of "Spy Game"
5. ___ up (shredded)
6. F.I.C.A. funds it
9. Myopic
10. Prefix with centric
11. Lacked, briefly
14. "Who'll Stop the Rain" band
16. Domestic machine: abbr.
19. Prefix with potent
21. Rotate
22. Grandma, to Germans
25. Centers for G.I.s, initially
26. Off-the-scale?
27. Paved the way (to): 2 wds.
29. Div. including the Phillies and Mets: 2 wds.
30. Tennis match starters
32. Having one sharp (music): 2 wds.
35. Activist
36. Artist Warhol
38. "Charlotte's Web" monogram

152

Across

1. "Brandenburg Concertos" composer
5. Ride, so to speak
11. Begrimed with soot
12. "Lawrence of ___"
13. Command
14. Converted, in a way
15. Animal house?
16. Amount in a Brylcreem slogan
17. Fall tool
19. Doctrines
23. Getting blocked with fine sand
26. "Stupid ___ Tricks" (Letterman bit)
27. Less cordial
28. Built round?
30. Big brute
31. Patella
33. C, for one
35. Fungal spore sacs
36. Bon ___
38. Boys
41. Elk
44. A little of this and a little of that dish
45. City north of Lisbon, Portugal
46. Arm bone
47. ___ Rockefeller, vice president under Ford
48. Gray remover, perhaps

Down

1. Event attended by Cinderella
2. Floating, perhaps
3. One way to get up a mountain
4. Supply water
5. Gel
6. Carpet layer's calculation
7. Browning's Ben Ezra, e.g.
8. Blood-typing letters
9. "Can I help you, ___?"
10. ___ Juan, P.R.
18. "Star Trek" captain
20. In particular
21. Elevated flat top, or an Arizona city
22. "___ lively!"
23. "Da Vinci Code" priory
24. U.N. flight agency
25. Says, to a teen
29. Make less visible, old-style
32. Land
34. Eastern V.I.P.s
37. "Beetle Bailey" barker
39. Banquet
40. Go paragliding, say
41. Came in first
42. Class clown, often
43. Party planner, for short?

153

Across

1 Brief shots?
5 "___ Joes" (boutique grocery store)
11 Desire analgesics, maybe
12 Bring back
13 Kaput, as a battery
14 Avoided, as the law
15 Bundle
17 Lawn mower's path
19 Physics units
22 "M*A*S*H" setting
23 Saloon fight
25 Get lost, say
26 Gary's role in "The Pride of the Yankees"
27 Alternatives to sandwiches
30 Bit of inspiration
32 Protomatter of the universe
33 "French Kiss" costar
34 Mixer
36 "I have found it" (Archimedes)
39 Back of the neck
42 Kitchen gadget
43 Ruler of Kuwait, e.g.
44 "___ and upward!"
45 Scotch ___ (adhesive)

Down

1 Groovy flat?
2 Rocks, at a bar
3 Thicket
4 Calm down
5 "Star ___" (Shatner show)
6 Studio effect, briefly
7 "The Hurt Locker" beat it for Best Picture
8 "___ not!"
9 "The Three Faces of ___"
10 Cabernet, e.g.
16 When doubled, a dance
17 Corrupt, as results of a test
18 Fret
20 Tibetan Buddhist chief: 2 wds.
21 Given an oath, with "in"
24 Gospel writer
28 100 centimos
29 Person who asks "Got a light?"
30 Enjoy a Winter Olympics sport
31 Earth, for one
35 Diamond, e.g.
36 An obnoxious person may have a large one
37 Ash cache
38 Crude
40 Dickens hero
41 Before, old-style

154

The grid:

Across

1 Datebook entry: abbr.
5 Attacks: 2 wds.
10 Clean up, in a way
12 Beneficial: 2 wds.
13 African language
14 ___ Carlo
15 Little pest
16 Ogles offensively: 2 wds.
18 Less likely to fall over
20 Princess, initially
21 Magnetic induction unit
22 Suffix for gran and graph
23 Beat the pants off
25 Stayed in a lodge
27 Howard of "Happy Days"
28 Scene of W.W. I fighting
30 Initially a port
31 Binds together: 2 wds.
34 Vulture's dinner?
36 "___ la la…"
37 Special way of doing something
38 Being broadcast: 2 wds.
40 Arise
41 Jottings
42 Irritates
43 Sandwich retailer

Down

1 Mahmoud ___, president of Palestine after Yasser Arafat
2 Industrial building
3 Senior military staff: 2 wds.
4 Vietnamese lunar New Year
5 Bart, Lisa and Maggie's dad: 2 wds.
6 Gets an ___ effort: 2 wds.
7 Florida: 2 wds.
8 Phoenician goddess of love and fertility
9 Grew biters
11 Go to live elsewhere: 3 wds.
17 Suffix with adopt or address
19 Suddenly
23 Long-distance driver
24 "Silverado" actress Arquette
26 Long-running UK music mag.
29 Alliance created in 1948, initially
32 Poem by Ralph Waldo Emerson
33 Adherent of Zoroastrianism
35 Bra size: 2 wds.
39 Affirmative action

155

Across

1. Like the "ng" sound
6. Boo-boo, to a tot
10. Sighed with delight
11. At right angles to the length of a plane
12. "Reversal of Fortune" star Jeremy
13. Publisher Henry and newsman Lester
14. Dream, in Paris
15. EZ Pass figure
16. Black billiard ball
18. Peyton Manning and Tom Brady, e.g.
21. Computer file container
23. Mary of "Where Eagles Dare"
24. First name in despotism
25. Also
27. ___ Lingus
28. Cariou of "Sweeney Todd"
29. Cub Scout leaders, in the U.K.
31. Not be up-to-date
32. East German secret police
33. Agile
35. Some G.I.s
38. ___ Delgada, E Azores
40. Every 24 hours
41. Lily family plants
42. "It's just ___ those things": 2 wds.
43. Bryn ___ College
44. Storage container

Down

1. "Precision Face & Upper Lip Kit" brand name
2. Bern's river
3. Kid's wintertime employment: 2 wds.
4. Virgil epic
5. The Mormon church, initially
6. Ancient Greek coin
7. Having the necessary expertise: hyph.
8. "Am ___ risk?": 2 wds.
9. Scrabble three-pointers
11. "Cat on ___ Tin Roof": 2 wds.
15. Hoarse, rasping
17. Affect, with "to"
19. Town north of Anaheim, California
20. Sun. talks?
21. Plug up
22. Concert sites
26. Semi-soft Canadian cheese
30. Owner of Menorca
32. Mrs.'s counterparts, in Mexico
34. Dino flyer's prefix
36. Blockhead
37. "Wynonna Earp" channel
38. One of TV's Ewings
39. Spanish wave
40. Medical practitioner, briefly

156

Across

1 Traditional theme, motif

6 Greek portico

10 ___ in (overflowing with)

11 Evil spirit

12 Seat of Greene County, Ohio

13 Became an issue

14 Certain system of highways

16 Turn red or yellow, say

17 Historical periods

20 Maker of chic shades

24 Toothed tool

25 African grazer

26 Before, before

27 Britney of pop

29 ___ moss

30 Supermodel Campbell

32 Restrained

37 Persian Gulf emirate

38 At hand

39 Seed coverings

40 Nigerian language

41 "All ___ are off!"

42 "As You Like It" setting

Down

1 2004 Queen Latifah movie

2 John Irving's "A Prayer for ___ Meany"

3 Breathe hard

4 Some willows

5 Emmy-winning Lewis

6 Got smaller

7 Horn sound

8 Any of three English rivers

9 Drink on draft

11 Rich cake

15 Champion

17 Biblical beast

18 Clothing store, with "The"

19 Green grass eater

21 "Malcolm X" director

22 Geologic time period

23 Anyhow

25 Free

28 Historical records

29 Means of support

31 Chocolate-coffee flavoring

32 Fix, as a medical condition

33 Brief bio, on parting

34 Clear's partner

35 To be, in old Rome

36 Torvill's skating partner

37 Apply gently

157

Across

1. Couples
6. Bacteria
11. Blue hue
12. Common daisy
13. Began to smoke: 2 wds.
14. Botherer
15. Eastern ties
17. Absorbs, with "up"
18. Animal represented in the zodiac by Aries
20. An empty bottle is full of it
22. Athletic supporter?
23. "Shoo!"
25. Study (with "over")
27. Festivals
29. Ball game
32. "___ of the Dead" (Karloff film)
34. Plane, e.g.
35. Cul-de-___
37. Be a chatterbox
39. "Yes" indication
40. Chesapeake Bay creature
42. Assay or essay, perhaps
44. Burning
46. They may have abs of stone
49. "Hello ___!"
50. Cool
51. Class
52. Hangs out

Down

1. City in Tex.
2. Action film staple
3. In an unthinking way
4. Clobber
5. Brown-tinted photo
6. Pan, e.g.
7. Donald and Ivana, e.g.
8. Channel changer: 2 wds.
9. Mr. Magoo, for one
10. "That makes no ___!"
16. Little bit, as of coffee
18. "A Yank in the ___" (1941 film)
19. Amaze
21. Bassist Wasserman
24. "Without question!"
26. "Baloney!"
28. Arch
30. Bill and ___
31. Antiquity, in antiquity
33. "___, drink, and be merry"
35. A lot
36. Cant
38. "She loves me not" determiner
41. ___ weevil
43. Aria, e.g.
45. English river
47. Another word for the Sun
48. Conditions

158

The grid:

1	2	3	4		5	6	7	8	9
10					11				
12				13					
14			15				16		
17			18			19			
20		21				22			
	23			24					
25	26			27			28	29	
30		31				32			
33		34				35			
36		37			38				
39					40				
41					42				

Across

1. Hate group
5. Smallville family
10. Zippo
11. O'clock, to Jacques
12. "By the powers vested ___...": 2 wds.
13. Ill will
14. 401, to Caesar
15. Perfect gymnastics score
16. Heavy-duty cleanser
17. Neb. neighbor
18. Out of date person or thing: hyph.
20. Looked good on
22. Unusual, in Caesar's day
23. Long, narrow bank at the mouth of a river
25. Part of NASA, briefly
27. Break
30. Pitching stats?: 2 wds.
32. To the ___ degree
33. When repeated, a dance
34. Dunderhead
35. Geologic time period
36. Throw (dice) again
38. Warm-up, briefly
39. Jagged, as a leaf's edge
40. "A Death in the Family" author
41. Feudal workers
42. "Blue" TV lawmen

Down

1. Madison Square Garden squad, familiarly
2. Actress Juliet, Drusilla on "Buffy the Vampire Slayer"
3. Business manager
4. Scot's refusal
5. Kublai, Genghis and Aly
6. Poetic time of day
7. Power station output, at times: 2 wds.
8. "Gnome Alone" star Verne
9. Venus's sister
13. Look at (a problem) once again
15. At that point
19. Bric-a-___
21. Currency of Western Samoa
24. Harry Truman's wife
25. Mother-of-pearl sources
26. Cleave
28. Meryl of "The Iron Lady"
29. Like topiary
31. Shocks with a device
37. Annual Ashland event, initially
38. Gold digger's prop

159

Across

1 Treble clef lines
6 First common carrier railroad: 3 wds.
11 Famed restaurateur Vincent
12 "Yond Cassius has ___ and hungry look": 2 wds.
13 Already in being: hyph.
15 Supermarket chain letters
16 Prefix with lingual or lateral
17 502, in Ancient Rome
18 Golfer Ernie, nicknamed "The Big Easy"
19 Suffix with event
20 Pro ___ (for now)
21 Blocks
23 Professional sportswriter and boxing expert Kevin
24 Coffee order
26 Some health professionals, initially
29 "Shining Through" writer Susan
33 Suffix with glob
34 19th Presidential initials
35 "___-Devil" (1989 Meryl Streep movie)
36 Little bird
37 Guidonian note
38 Prince, to a king
39 Hearty repasts: 2 wds.
42 Mea ___
43 Roman magistrate responsible for public buildings
44 "Sunset Boulevard" Tony winner George
45 Part of a religious title

Down

1 Saw
2 Use Betadine, e.g.
3 Chicken serving
4 Cold War monogram
5 Object that is permanently in place
6 So-called "royal herb"
7 Computer key that's usually next to the space bar
8 Must: 2 wds.
9 1973 Elton John hit
10 Promptly: 2 wds.
14 Quick-tempered
22 Asner and Bradley
23 "___ Man Answers" (1962 Bobby Darin song): 2 wds.
25 Red with embarrassment
26 Violent attempt to overthrow a government
27 Exclusive circle of people
28 Singer Clark
30 Go after violently
31 Spiny cactus
32 Japanese teacher
34 Aired a second time
40 Mo. whose birthstone is the diamond
41 Author LeShan

160

Across

1 Leaves of a book
6 Indolent
10 N.F.L. Hall-of-Famer Hirsch
11 Dusk, old-style
12 Fertile soil
13 Rinse, as with a solvent
14 Suffix with cap or coy
15 Revival producer?: inits.
17 "It's cold!"
18 Pop's boy
19 Sch. in Tulsa, Oklahoma
20 52, in old Rome
21 "___ Came Back Again" (Johnny Cash song): 2 wds.
23 Temper, as metal
25 Five Nations members
27 Mountain lion
29 Narrow-waisted stinger
32 Online feed, initially
33 Fix, as a fight
35 Conflict
36 Flying expert
37 ___-Bilt (power tool brand)
38 Letters on some invitations
39 Great: prefix
41 Sewing cases
43 Civil War general defeated by Grant at Chattanooga
44 First five of 26
45 Skeleton part, in Padua
46 Powerful sharks

Down

1 First female House Speaker
2 Many: 3 wds.
3 Carbon dioxide, e.g.: 2 wds.
4 Selene's sister
5 Major food service company
6 "___ say!"
7 Twenty dollar bill, slangily: 2 wds.
8 Supreme worship allowed to God alone
9 Chef Lagasse who says "Pork fat rules!"
11 Coming or going, e.g.
16 Large open area of grassland
22 Chang's Siamese twin
24 "I don't think so"
26 Small elongated insect
27 Rhyming word game
28 Hollywood awards
30 Get married: 3 wds.
31 Non-poetic writing forms
34 Shine
40 First president of South Vietnam, ___ Dinh Diem
42 Not yet decided, initially

161

Across

1. Dead, as an engine
6. Emulate a litterbug
11. ___ Jeane Baker (Marilyn Monroe's real name)
12. ___ rhythm, brain waves pattern
13. All thumbs
14. Indemnify
15. Gumshoe, for short
16. More even
18. ___ of Langerhans
20. ___ grass
23. Emulated running mates?
25. "Great" dog
26. Rains hard
27. Post-skiing beverage, for some
28. "___ Street" ("Annie" song)
29. Hawaiian welcomes
30. "Star Trek" rank: abbr.
31. Cold-weather wear
32. ___ pole
34. "La Femme Nikita" network
37. Exceeding
39. Sweater material
41. Corporal punishment inflictor
42. Fixed the pilot
43. In that place
44. What's in, in fashion

Down

1. Jersey, e.g.
2. Top-grade: hyph.
3. Emerald or sapphire, e.g.
4. Short strike caller?
5. Rats
6. Pompous walk
7. "With this ring, I ___ wed"
8. In a reproving manner
9. H, to Homer
10. Kind of station
17. Color on China's flag
19. Active
21. Relative of the buffalo
22. Green and herb, e.g.
23. Foil alternative
24. Advance
25. "Let's Make a Deal" offering
27. Blares
29. Great serve, in tennis
31. About 1.3 cubic yards
33. "One Flew ___ The Cuckoo's Nest" (1975)
35. Agronomy concern
36. A chip, maybe
37. Appear
38. "___, humbug!"
40. Abbr. after some generals' names

162

Across

1 Some Italian cars, for short
6 Clenched hands
11 Sierra ___
12 Jellied garnish
13 Like ghost stories
14 100 kobo in Nigeria
15 Breaks off
17 Part of a list
18 Avoid
19 Alternative to a fence
21 Voting "nay"
22 Deliberately invalid but ingenious argument
25 Exist en masse
26 "That means ___!"
27 Prefix with classical
28 Takes back a former statement
30 Serengeti grazer
31 "That hurt!"
32 Commend
33 Macbeth, for one
35 Hindu religious teacher
37 Caulking fiber
39 Arboreal animal
41 Word before suspect or rate
42 Earnings
43 Exhausted, as resources
44 Grave marker

Down

1 Draft choice
2 Coast that the wind blows on: 2 wds.
3 Baked dough cake containing a prediction: 2 wds.
4 Charged particle
5 Percolate
6 Buff
7 "Two Concepts of Liberty" author Berlin
8 Exact double of another: 2 wds.
9 Radial, e.g.
10 Dishonest way to make money
16 Irons out creases
18 Animated Disney villain
20 Big production
22 Coordinate
23 Guard
24 Grimace of discontent
29 Fall in Britain
32 Diamond weight
33 Soaks (up), as with a paper towel
34 Gripe
36 Impresses greatly
38 Came across
40 Fed. property overseer

163

Across

1 California vineyard valley
5 Desert bloomers
10 Completely: 2 wds.
12 Like an egg
13 They hide the ends of roof timbers
15 Eastern music
16 E.U. member, shortly
17 Cry of surprise
19 Nimble, like a gymnast
21 Figure out
22 PC linkup
23 1965 Ursula Andress film
26 W.W. II fighter pilots' gp.
27 Fractional ending
28 Twaddle
29 Important time
30 Baltic or Irish
31 Lode load
32 Fragrance
34 Born, in France
35 Chinese brew
36 Heap praise upon
38 Insignificant amount (of money): 2 wds.
42 "Jane Eyre" character, Grace ____
43 Country, capital Nuku'alofa
44 Sleeping concern
45 Load up

Down

1 Point
2 Santa ____, California
3 By rote: hyph.
4 Aquatic plant
5 Loving murmur
6 Benefit
7 Person who writes letters on a regular basis
8 Low or high
9 Bouncers ask for them
11 Courtroom jargon
14 Thing of little importance
17 Fairy-tale character
18 Try, as a case
20 Asthmatic's aid
24 Relative of a rabbit
25 Fencing sword
33 Mineral discoloration
35 Karate move
37 Vehicles initially from outer space?
38 Tax worker, initially
39 Mauna ____
40 It may be easily bruised
41 Margery of rhyme

164

Across

1 End of "Coriolanus": 2 wds.
5 "Way of the gods," literally
11 "Boss Lady" star Lynn
12 ___ hearts (red playing card): 2 wds.
13 Pennsylvanian city known as "The Gem City"
14 Pontiac, e.g.
15 Workout wear
17 Geological ridge
18 Cool eyewear
21 Cutlet?
25 Coffee-to-go need
26 Ballerina's pivot point
27 Acted like
29 Auteur's art
32 Finnish architect Alvar ___
34 Bruce Willis film: 2 wds.
39 Latin-American dances
40 "Able was I ___ saw Elba": 2 wds.
41 Adjust
42 Cash advance
43 Chemical cousin
44 First video game

Down

1 Biblical shepherd
2 Attention
3 H.S. math
4 Watched
5 Underwater toons of the 1980s
6 Words to a blackjack dealer: 2 wds.
7 Unpaid worker, often
8 Impending
9 Drags
10 "Son ___ gun!": 2 wds.
16 Widow in "Peer Gynt"
18 Hearst kidnap grp.
19 Edgy
20 Drink suffix
22 Mineral suffix
23 Dot follower
24 Mauna ___, Hawaii
28 "Consarn it, ye varmint!"
29 Deal maker
30 BBC rival
31 Useless
33 All together: 2 wds.
34 Bowlers, e.g.
35 "___us a son…"
36 Slangy suffix for "buck"
37 Withdraw gradually
38 Card in a royal flush
39 "___-Pan" (1966 novel)

165

Across

1 Mus. chord: 2 wds.

5 Tastelessly showy in manner

11 Bring down

12 Charge: 2 wds.

13 "Look ___ Now, Mother!" (Gayle Kirschenbaum movie of 2015): 2 wds.

14 Deaden

15 Major road or highway

17 Bliss

22 Mustard family member

26 French girl, briefly

27 Non-reactive, like some gases

28 Entire range

29 "I Wish" rapper ___-Lo

30 My friend, in Marseilles: 2 wds.

31 Automobile safety device: 2 wds.

33 Accelerated a motor, casually

38 Movie of someone's life

42 Change

43 Cotton fabric

44 Cut short

45 Heart implants

46 Improve, as acting skills

Down

1 What the suspicious may smell: 2 wds.

2 S.A.T. section

3 Cote d'___

4 "___, Joy of Man's Desiring"

5 Bring up (as a topic)

6 Dee and Dandridge

7 Curaçao clock setting letters

8 Egyptian god of light and air

9 ___ Bernardino

10 Col. in a profit-and-loss statement

16 Left on the map

18 Bad bill collector?: hyph.

19 "Brokeback Mountain" heroine

20 Inner-city blight

21 Bigfoot's Asian cousin

22 Specialized computer, for short

23 "Diana" crooner

24 Tick's host, maybe

25 Fits of rage

28 Don't skip: 2 wds.

30 Imelda or Ferdinand

32 Expel a tenant

34 Gp. of musicians

35 Prefix with dramatic

36 Scottish capital, briefly

37 Blockhead

38 N.C.A.A. football ranking system

39 "Can ___ least sit down?": 2 wds.

40 "___ Buttermilk Sky" (Hoagy Carmichael song)

41 Jewelry box item

166

Across

1 Computer programming language, initially
6 Flog ___ horse: 2 wds.
11 Chicago Bears coaching legend Mike
12 Fab, in showbiz lingo
13 Spot seller, for short: 2 wds.
14 Awaiting: 2 wds.
15 Senatorial affirmative
16 Country in Eur.
18 Erstwhile radio duo, ___ and Abner
19 F.I.C.A. benefit
20 Professor's helpers, initially
21 Ending for pay or gran
22 More than willing
24 "East of Eden" twin
25 "Over There" composer George M. ___
27 Split
28 "Star Wars" name
29 ___ Tavern ("The Simpsons" locale)
30 Raiding grp.
31 New age chant
32 Welsh mountain valley
35 College founded by Thomas Jefferson, initially
36 Clothing flaw
37 Suffix with mock
38 Winter warmer
40 Everything, to Caesar
42 Kindle material: hyph.
43 Table of contents page, often
44 Color anew
45 12-year-old, say

Down

1 Times to give gifts, briefly
2 Gofers
3 Having a serious expression: hyph.
4 Alibi guy
5 Cylinder used for winding a cable
6 Broadway's "___ Irish Rose"
7 Cheadle or King
8 Powdery deposit on a surface
9 In conflict with: 2 wds.
10 Idle
17 Ball of cotton
23 Midback muscle, for short
24 Drink on draft
25 "Canterbury Tales" author Geoffrey
26 Beat, in a way
27 Behave
29 2001, to Nero
31 Practice public speaking
33 Correspond
34 "...And—which is more—you'll be a Man, ___" (Kipling): 2 wds.
39 Prefix with acetylene
41 Copy cats?

167

Across

1 Top-40 DJ Casey
6 Actors Tim and Daphne Maxwell
11 Nicholas Gage best seller
12 "Ready ___ ...": 2 wds.
13 Honeydew, e.g.
14 Raison ___
15 Treasury Dept. branch
16 Chemical ending
18 AIDS cause
19 Lake: Fr.
20 "Liquor not provided" letters
21 Summer: Fr.
22 Sonata, e.g.
24 "Chacun ___ goÛt": 2 wds.
25 Drainage site
27 Music Appreciation, for one
28 "Knight Rider" star's nickname, with "The"
29 ___ Sunday
30 Charlotte to Raleigh dir.
31 Phil Rizzuto, on the Yankees
32 Clinton ___
35 Refrigerator letters, sometimes
36 Newman title role of 1963
37 Tennessee athlete, for short
38 Actor Davis of "Do the Right Thing"
40 "Boy, Did ___ Wrong Number!" (1966 movie): 3 wds.
42 Chemical prefix
43 Bana and Bogosian
44 Flaps: hyph.
45 "Eternal Sunshine of the Spotless Mind" actress Kirsten

Down

1 Turkey's Atatürk
2 Prince Valiant's wife
3 Owned up to: hyph.
4 Rocker Brian
5 Small coach
6 Cowboy's event
7 Afore
8 Similar: 4 wds.
9 Chip company with the tagline "For the bold"
10 Wallace ___, Pulitzer Prize winning poet
17 "Bad" beginning
23 Sta-___ fabric softener
24 Everyone
25 Nanny, for one: 2 wds.
26 "The Bald Soprano" playwright
27 Coated with sugar
29 Little, in Lille
31 TV's Huxtable and Kojak, for two
33 Univ. military programs
34 Make ___-ditch effort: 2 wds.
39 "How was ___ know?": 2 wds.
41 Steve Carell's "Despicable Me" character

168

Across

1. Speaks
6. Part of a Spanish play
10. Eastern Catholic
11. Animal with a horn, briefly
13. Bride in Barcelona
14. Off the plate, maybe
15. Computer file suffix
16. Cast a spell over
18. Put out of action
20. Neighbor of a Vietnamese
21. What's not hurt, in idiom: 2 wds.
22. "Dead ___" (Dick Francis mystery)
23. Experienced sailor, familiarly: 2 wds.
25. Pol. divisions prior to 1991
27. Corp. official
29. Kindergartner
30. Italian dish cooked with broth
32. Manufacture
34. Credit-tracking corp., once
35. "As You Like It" setting
36. "Believe me, that's ___": 2 wds.
38. "I love you," to Maria: 2 wds.
39. "In other words…": 2 wds.
40. Capital of Rhône
41. Relinquishes

Down

1. Fixed a piano
2. It may cause a coma
3. Doesn't plan with an eye to the future: 3 wds.
4. China's Chiang ___-shek
5. Ran through
6. "___ Done Yet?" (movie starring Ice Cube): 2 wds.
7. Spicy coffeehouse order
8. Gossiped idly: hyph.
9. Like some garages, size-wise: hyph.
12. "… ___ coals," firewalking phrase: 2 wds.
17. Stretchy
19. Whittier poem "___ Well"
22. Basset hound on TV's "The People's Choice"
24. Popular poison in whodunits
25. March honoree, familiarly: 2 wds.
26. Reddish brown color
28. Fine furrows
30. Chatter: 2 wds.
31. Buck of "Hee Haw"
33. Sample
37. Cockney dwelling

169

Across

1 That woman
4 Mountain like the Matterhorn
7 Golfer's goal
10 Dinghy mover
11 Canned fish
13 Situations that could suddenly become violent
15 Nonsense
16 Puppy's foot
17 Egyptian snake
20 Jerk: var.
23 Farfalle pasta shape: 2 wds.
26 Glasses holder
27 One of Ten in the Bible
29 Director ____ Howard
30 Corporeal, physical
31 H.S. math
33 Big Apple inits.
34 Promise
36 Flat floater
40 Morbid fear of open spaces
44 Divine
45 To do it is human
46 One of a foot's five
47 ____ and cheese sandwich
48 Kind of square or shirt

Down

1 Delicate
2 Saintly glow
3 Baseball stats.
4 Cigar stuff
5 Drink like a dog
6 Item on a stage
7 Child's toy that turns in the wind
8 Aardvark's snack
9 Lo-____
12 First European to round the Cape of Good Hope
14 Medieval oboe
18 Bayonet
19 Nut-bearing conifer
21 Myriad
22 Uneaten morsel
23 Philistine
24 Eater of meat and vegetables
25 Mary Baker ____
27 PC monitor type
28 Prefix with scope or economics
32 He came after Quayle
35 Laundry load
37 Aid in crime
38 Conflagration
39 Weight not charged for
40 Naval direction
41 Sentimental drivel
42 Princess tormentor
43 Haw's partner

170

The grid:

```
 1  2  3  4  5  ██  6  7  8  9 10
11           ██ 12
13           ██ 14
██     15       16       ██ 17
18 19        20       ██ 21
22      23       ██    24    25 26
27           ██ 28
29           ██ 30
██     31       32       ██ 33
34 35        36       ██ 37
38      39       ██ 40       41 42
43           ██ 44
45           ██ 46
```

Across

1 Combat gear
6 Humidor item
11 "Dona Flor and Her Two Husbands" author Jorge
12 John Cougar's "___ So Good"
13 Former coins of India
14 Apple desktops
15 Syrian leader
17 Santa's shouts
18 Feel like a ___ in the machine
20 "The Faerie Queene" character
22 Bard's stage direction
24 "I ___ top of the world!": 2 wds.
27 "Goodfellas" actor
28 Crazy person, slangily
29 Hydroxyl compound
30 "Batman" butler
31 ___ Kea, Hawaiian peak
33 Drink dunked on Super Bowl-winning coaches, often
34 Rap group based in Southern Chicago
36 Cul-___, dead-end street: 2 wds.
38 "Chicago Hope" actress
40 Snaps
43 Nutmeg state school, briefly
44 Chicago's ___ Expressway
45 "Chinatown" screenwriter Robert
46 Harder to locate

Down

1 Jump provider, initially
2 L.B.J. follower
3 Persist despite hardship: 2 wds.
4 Sultana's chambers
5 "Semiramide" composer
6 Scold
7 Ending for titan or thor
8 Whole wheat wafer: 2 wds.
9 Early record label for Bobby Darin and the Beatles
10 Letters for distributing news to Web users
16 Cunning
18 Edible European mushroom: var.
19 Anoas and gaurs
21 Innocent
23 Arthur Ashe's alma mater, in short
25 Sanctioned, briefly
26 Central point
28 Horror movie genre, slangily
30 Hydrocarbon suffix
32 City near Venice
34 Overabundance
35 ___ Noir (hybrid red wine grape)
37 "O patria mia" singer
39 Basic cable channel
41 Ethyl or acetyl ender
42 Old geographical inits.

171

Across

1   Willing to face danger
6   Aircraft controller
11 Wise words
12 Accused's need
13 Criminal mobs
14 Fey
15 "The L Word" actress Daniels
16 Beer amount
17 Warm dry mountain wind: var.
19 Adept
22 Horse, to a child: hyph.
24 Criticize
25 "Rumor ____ it..."
26 Place for a cat, often
28 Gay Nineties, e.g.
29 "Humanum ____ errare"
30 Decorative bunch of cords
32 ____ Aquarids (meteor shower associated with Halley's Comet)
33 Like many Poe stories
34 Boris Godunov, for one
36 Misdeals, e.g.
39 Cream and The Police, for two
41 Blacksmith's block
42 ____ dark space (region in a vacuum tube)
43 Give extreme unction, once
44 Clichéd
45 Ran quick

Down

1   Plum variety
2   Jewish calendar's sixth month
3   Appearance in bodily form, as of a ghost
4   Christmas drink
5   "Absolutely!"
6   Song of joy
7   Pollution, poverty, etc.
8   Flotation device: 2 wds.
9   "Kill Bill" sash
10 Only three-letter element
16 Crook
18 Fish that can be "electric"
20 Collector's guide adjective
21 Girasol, e.g.
22 Clarified butter in Indian cookery
23 "____ of Eden"
27 Golf course score
31 Burnt ____ (Crayola color)
33 Artist's stand
35 Pop, to some
37 Anger, with "up"
38 "Mush!" shouter's vehicle
39 Bill
40 Part of a cell nucleus, briefly
41 "How very nice!"

172

Across

1 Fever
5 High-kicking dance of French origin
11 "___ want for Christmas ...": 2 wds.
12 "How to Steal a Million" star Peter
13 Resourceful, enterprising
15 Famous advice from Horace Greeley: 2 wds.
16 Take out ___ in the paper (publicize): 2 wds.
17 Cry of a wild goose
19 "___ Not Gonna Take It"
23 Short coat
27 Where to see stars indoors
29 "The Jungle Book" boy
30 Lat., Rus., and Ukr., once
31 "Right Now (Na Na Na)" rapper
33 Bit of kindling
36 Pyle player Jim
41 1901 Kentucky Derby winner: 2 wds.
43 Annual showbiz awards
44 Cord fiber
45 Gift giver's command: 2 wds.
46 Proof of purchase: abbr.

Down

1 Former Defense Secretary Alexander
2 Red Muppet
3 "There oughta be ___ ...": 2 wds.
4 Buster Brown's dog
5 Acrobat who adopts unusual postures
6 One day ___ time: 2 wds.
7 "Isn't anyone interested?": 2 wds.
8 Quarter, e.g.
9 Edison's middle name
10 Requirement
14 "Sort of" suffix
18 King Features competitor
19 Secretarial speed, for short
20 "Hold On Tight" group letters
21 Crude
22 Participate: 2 wds.
24 Hi-___, certain LP players
25 Belgium's continent: abbr.
26 Apt. ad info.
28 Animal on Michigan's flag
32 A Bobbsey twin
33 "The Cosby Show" boy
34 Chicken
35 "This ___" (Randy Travis album): 2 wds.
37 The Home Depot paint brand
38 A hundred bucks: 2 wds.
39 Dudley Do-Right's gp.
40 Aug. follower
42 "___ want a hula hoop..." (Chipmunks): 2 wds.

173

Across

1 City near the Ruhr and Rhine
6 Post-Manhattan Project org.
9 "War Dances" writer Sherman
11 Garage event
12 Economize
13 Web page addresses, initially
14 Sandy Nelson instrumental song of 1959: 2 wds.
16 Own
18 Numero uno
19 Playground device
23 Eyeball-bending genre: 2 wds.
25 Kind of paper
26 Doctor's request: 2 wds.
28 ___ the Impaler (Dracula prototype)
29 Trifling
31 No-show
34 "The Witches" director Nicolas
35 Threaten
39 "Knowledge can split ___ of light" (Dickens): 2 wds.
40 Bible book after Proverbs: abbr.
41 School of whales
42 "The Family Circus" cartoonist Bil

Down

1 Federal warning system activated by FEMA
2 Utah's capital, initially
3 To be, in Barcelona
4 Preplanned means of escape: 2 wds.
5 Gard department capital
6 Sight from Bern
7 Actress Raines
8 "It is" to Pierre
10 Foils
11 Obsequiousness
15 One sixty-billionth of a min.: 2 wds.
16 Music's Salt 'N' ___
17 "___ can you see": 2 wds.
18 Mass. city
20 Ward of "Sisters"
21 "Come on, be ___!": 2 wds.
22 Got hitched
24 Small mountain lake
27 Request of a card dealer: 2 wds.
30 "Sport Shirt Bill"
31 As limp as ___: 2 wds.
32 When repeated, an island NW of Tahiti
33 Tailor's stitch
36 Miss. neighbor
37 Long time: abbr.
38 Vane dir.

SOLUTIONS

1

B	I	P	E	D			O	R	F	F	
I	S	E	R	E		M	E	R	L	E	
C	O	R	R	E	L	A	T	I	O	N	
			I	S	P	S		E	D	U	C
E	D	O		S	A	P		G	R	O	
A	U	D	I	O	T	A	P	E			
P	O	I	L	U		R	A	F	T	S	
		C	A	T	H	E	D	R	A	L	
U	L	T		H	A	G		E	E	R	
S	O	A	P		R	O	V	E			
N	O	B	E	L	P	R	I	Z	E	S	
R	I	L	K	E		I	T	E	R	3	
	E	E	E	S		C	A	R	A	T	

2

I	C	B	M			F	A	U	N	A	
C	O	R	A		D	O	L	L	E	D	
A	D	A	R		R	O	U	T	E	D	
O	A	S	T		E	L	M				
			S	E	A	S		N	I	S	I
D	O	I	N	G	S		A	M	P	S	
I	V	E		A	C	E		M	E	N	
V	E	R	B		I	N	S	E	C	T	
A	R	E	A		R	E	E	D			
			A	R	C		L	I	S	P	
S	E	R	I	A	L		L	A	I	R	
A	V	E	N	G	E		E	T	N	A	
W	E	D	G	E			R	E	S	T	

3

R	A	S	E		A	C	T	O	N	E	
A	R	U	G		V	O	Y	E	U	R	
R	I	G	G		U	N	P	O	T	S	
A	D	A	H		L	G	E				
			R	E	E	S		B	B	L	S
R	E	L	A	X	E	S		O	I	L	
E	R	O	D	E		H	A	R	P	O	
A	G	A		C	O	M	E	N	O	W	
R	O	F	L		S	O	R	T			
			Y	R	S		I	O	L	A	
S	A	N	S	E	I		A	R	Y	L	
R	A	N	O	F	F		I	U	R	E	
S	H	E	L	T	Y		S	N	E	E	

4

S	L	E	E	V	E	S					
I	I	N	S	I	S	T		L	B	O	
D	E	F	A	L	C	A	T	I	O	N	
E	R	R			E	D	E	N	I	C	
S	N	A	P	S		T	R	E	N	D	
	E	N	A	C	T		S	I	G	S	
		C	R	I	C	K	E	T			
E	C	H	O		P	I	L	E	S		
R	A	I	L	S		M	Y	M	A	N	
U	P	S	E	T	S			V	I	A	
P	R	E	D	I	C	A	M	E	N	T	
T	I	D		P	A	L	E	T	T	E	
			E	N	G	R	O	S	S		

5

C	A	R	B	O			T	O	S	S	
A	T	E	A	M		D	I	R	T	Y	
B	O	T	H	E	R	A	T	I	O	N	
A	N	I		G	E	E		O	N	O	
L	A	N		A	I	M		L	E	D	
S	L	A	T		N	O	S	E	D		
			W	A	S	N	T				
	S	N	O	U	T		Y	L	E	M	
S	E	A		P	A	D		A	Y	E	
H	I	P		A	T	E		M	E	T	
I	N	A	L	I	E	N	A	B	L	E	
V	E	L	A	R		E	I	D	E	R	
A	R	M	Y			B	L	A	T	S	

6

R	E	C	T	O		S	E	R	B	S	
S	N	O	O	P		O	X	I	D	E	
V	E	L	D	T		N	A	C	R	E	
			L	O	I	S		M	O	M	A
U	S	A		C	O	S	I				
S	O	P	H		B	O	N	B	O	N	
C	A	S	A	S		L	E	O	N	A	
G	R	E	W	U	P		R	B	I	S	
			T	E	A	K		O	N	T	
T	A	N	H		R	E	P	L			
A	S	S	O	C		E	F	I	L	E	
R	E	F	R	Y		L	U	N	G	E	
P	A	W	N	S			Y	I	K	E	S

7

R	H	O	D	A			T	A	T	U	
E	A	S	E	L		O	L	I	N	S	
M	R	M	O	O	N	L	I	G	H	T	
I	D	O		O	I	D		R	U	E	
T	I	N	A	F	E	Y		I	R	T	
S	T	D	S		T	O	A	S	T	S	
			A	B	Z	U	G				
M	E	S	S	R	S		R	A	M	S	
A	V	A		E	C	L	O	G	U	E	
Y	E	P		E	H	S		N	N	E	
S	N	O	O	Z	E	A	L	A	R	M	
T	E	R	S	E		T	O	T	O	E	
	D	S	O	S		S	P	E	E	D	

8

W	S	J		C	G	I					
E	E	O		C	R	O		P	E	C	
E	T	H	I	C	A	L		E	N	L	
P	O	N	D		P	A	T	R	I	A	
E	F	F	A	C	E		E	S	A	S	
R	F	K		O	S	T	R	I	C	H	
			E	M	P	O	R	I	A		
S	A	N	T	A	F	E		N	H	A	
H	A	N	G		W	E	D	G	E	S	
O	N	E	E	A	R		R	U	I	N	
A	D	D		A	A	M	I	L	N	E	
T	E	Y		A	T	E		F	E	W	
			A	H	H						

9

D	E	M	O	B		C	A	C	H	E	
S	P	A	N	O		O	B	E	S	E	
M	E	G	A	N		O	R	R	I	S	
S	E	N		E	R	N	I	E			
			E	R	D	O	S		A	D	E
F	U	T	U	R	E		S	L	E	D	
U	N	I	T	Y		S	L	A	S	H	
M	U	C	H		S	K	U	N	K	S	
E	M	F		W	E	I	R	D			
		I	N	A	L	L		M	I	A	
P	L	E	A	D		L	A	I	R	S	
S	O	L	I	D		E	C	L	A	T	
S	A	D	L	Y		T	A	K	E	R	

10

S	A	B	R	E		S	N	A	P	S	
I	L	L	E	R		T	O	B	I	T	
P	L	A	T	A		E	L	E	N	A	
E	A	S	Y	S	T	R	E	E	T		
			P	E	O	N	S				
T	O	R	E	R	O		S	E	E	A	
S	A	D		S	T	L		S	E	A	
R	S	S	S		S	E	T	T	E	E	
			W	A	I	T	E				
	S	P	A	R	E	P	A	R	T	S	
B	E	A	N	O		A	R	I	A	L	
I	V	I	E	S		S	A	C	R	A	
D	E	D	E	E		S	T	O	N	Y	

11

B	I	B			U	N	W	E	P	T	
O	P	E	D		N	O	O	N	E	S	
O	S	S	O		C	H	O	O	S	E	
M	A	P	U	T	O						
			A	G	E	N	A		B	O	S
O	N	T	H	E	Q	T		R	K	O	
N	O	T	Y	O	U	R	C	A	L	L	
D	R	E		F	E	E	L	S	A	D	
E	A	R		F	R	A	U	S			
			A	T	E	A	S	E			
I	N	A	T	U	B		I	R	A	E	
F	O	R	M	A	L		N	D	A	K	
A	D	M	I	R	E			S	R	S	

12

L	U	C	C	I			D	E	A	R	
U	B	O	A	T	S		Y	A	R	E	
M	I	N	N	I	E		E	S	N	E	
			S	A	N	A		T	O	S	
Y	A	T		A	S	L	A	N			
A	G	E	D		C	A	R	O	L	E	
Y	U	R	I	G	A	G	A	R	I	N	
S	A	N	D	A	L		M	T	N	S	
			A	I	S	L	E		H	A	E
B	L	T			O	T	O	E			
O	E	I	L		P	A	D	A	U	K	
P	O	O	P		S	I	E	S	T	A	
S	I	N	N			L	A	T	E	N	

178

SOLUTIONS

13

S	T	R	U	T		C	R	A	V	E
W	O	O	S	H		H	E	M	I	N
O	U	T	E	R		A	L	E	C	S
P	R	E	D	E	S	T	I	N	E	
			T	E	P	E	E			
T	A	C	O		O	A	F	I	S	H
S	K	A		G	N	U		C	O	O
P	A	T	H	O	S		B	E	L	T
	A	D	O	R	E					
C	A	R	D	R	E	A	D	E	R	
H	O	R	D	E		A	N	O	D	E
A	R	I	E	S		L	I	V	I	D
J	E	A	N	S		M	E	E	T	S

14

M	A	S	T		A	G	L	E	A	M
E	G	E	R		C	R	E	A	S	E
L	U	C	I		H	E	A	L	T	H
C	E	R	A	M	I	S	T			
			E	L	E	E		H	I	G	H
E	N	T		A	R	S	E	N	I	O
Y	E	A	R	N		O	R	A	L	E
C	U	R	E	A	L	L		U	A	R
K	E	Y	S		A	V	I	D		
			P	A	N	E	L	I	S	T
T	A	K	I	N	G		I	B	A	R
L	A	O	T	S	E		A	L	D	A
C	A	R	E	E	R		D	E	E	S

15

W	A	U	G	H		T	A	P	E	S
A	P	N	E	A		S	W	O	R	E
S	P	I	L	L		P	L	U	M	P
T	A	N	D	E	M		S	N	I	T
E	L	F		Y	A	M		D	N	A
S	L	O	B		T	A	S	S	E	L
		R	A	T	A	T	A	T		
R	A	M	R	O	D		P	E	T	S
E	R	A		T	O	N		R	H	O
A	C	T	S		R	O	L	L	E	R
M	A	I	L	S		R	A	I	S	E
E	N	V	O	I		M	I	N	I	S
D	E	E	P	S		A	N	G	S	T

16

G	A	M	U	T		D	A	R	E	
A	C	U	T	E		E	C	O	L	E
R	E	L	A	X		B	R	Y	C	E
C	R	T		A	M	A		A	I	L
O	B	I		S	T	U		L	D	S
N	I	N	O		A	C	T	H		
	C	A	L	C		H	E	I	R	
		T	S	A	R		N	G	O	S
P	S	I		B	A	Y		H	O	C
E	L	O		O	F	A		N	T	H
D	A	N	N	O		W	H	E	L	M
I	V	A	N	S		P	A	S	E	O
	E	L	E	E		S	Y	S	T	S

17

S	T	O	A		H	E	A	R	S	E
I	O	N	S		Y	E	S	M	A	N
P	I	T	S		D	O	W	S	E	D
E	L	H	I		R	C	A			
		E	S	P	O		N	E	E	R
D	E	S	I	R	E	S		N	R	A
I	D	I		O	L	E		D	E	T
A	I	D		P	E	R	T	E	S	T
N	E	E	T		C	E	R	A		
			E	D	T		A	V	I	S
C	A	S	P	E	R		I	O	T	A
M	E	D	I	C	I		T	R	O	I
A	C	I	D	I	C		S	S	N	S

18

C	L	A	D		P	E	G	L	E	G
H	I	V	E		A	U	R	O	R	A
O	M	I	T		W	R	O	N	G	S
C	O	V	E	R	N	O	T	E	S	
				C	H	E	S	T		
T	I	P	T	O	E		O	P	A	L
A	C	E						O	V	A
B	E	A	R		S	A	L	T	E	D
			A	P	P	L	E			
	I	N	T	E	R	E	S	T	E	D
P	O	E	T	R	Y		S	A	R	I
A	T	E	A	S	E		E	R	I	N
D	A	R	T	E	R		R	O	E	S

19

R	S	V	P		A	L	G	A	E
A	L	E	E		S	A	L	L	Y
L	A	R	G	E	S	C	A	L	E
E	S	S		S	E	E	D		
S	H	O	O	T	S		E	A	S	E
		L	E	S	S		B	O	W	
T	R	A	D	E		A	B	A	T	E
S	O	L		M	A	M	A			
P	E	E	R		C	O	R	P	S	E
		O	P	U	S		A	I	R	
	A	U	T	O	M	A	T	I	O	N
D	R	O	N	E		O	N	U	S	
S	I	R	E	N		N	E	X	T	

20

S	T	O	I	C		A	C	E	R	B
T	E	R	R	A		L	O	V	E	R
O	S	I	E	R		D	R	A	P	E
U	T	E		A	L	E		C	O	W
P	A	L	A	V	E	R		U	S	E
			L	A	C		D	E	E	D
	C	O	U	N	T	R	I	E	S	
C	A	L	M		E	A	R			
O	D	D		B	R	I	T	I	S	H
H	E	M		I	N	N		D	O	E
E	N	A	T	E		B	A	L	L	S
I	C	I	E	R		O	G	E	E	S
R	E	D	E	S		W	O	R	S	E

21

S	P	R	A	G		S	A	G	O
T	I	A	R	A	S		E	L	A	N
A	K	I	M	B	O		L	O	G	E
Y	E	N		U	N	L	E	S	S	
			D	E	B	R	I	S		
A	B	R	E	A	S	T		A	F	T
T	R	O	L	L		W	A	I	L	S
M	A	P		S	T	I	R	R	U	P
			C	A	R	T	E	L		
S	A	L	A	M	I			I	M	P
E	S	A	U		B	E	A	N	I	E
T	H	U	S		E	L	D	E	S	T
H	Y	D	E		M	O	R	E	S	

22

A	B	E	S		A	R	I	S	T	A
R	O	L	E		L	A	N	I	N	A
A	L	L	A		S	V	E	L	T	E
M	E	A	N	S	T	E	S	T	S	
			C	O	O	L	S			
E	A	S	E	I	N		E	D	I	E
A	A	A						A	R	K
P	S	T	S		C	L	E	E	S	E
		T	R	E	E	R				
	S	P	R	I	N	G	R	O	L	L
S	E	R	I	F	S		A	L	A	E
I	C	I	C	L	E		T	A	C	T
G	O	I	T	E	R		A	V	E	O

23

S	C	A	L	P		P	L	A	S	M
H	O	N	E	Y		H	E	N	C	E
E	N	T	E	R	T	A	I	N	E	R
I	C	E		E	A	R		A	N	I
K	E	N	S		T	A	B	L	E	T
H	A	N	K		S	O	L			
S	L	A	I	N		H	I	R	E	D
			R	O	B		N	O	N	E
S	T	A	T	U	E		G	U	L	P
P	A	L		R	A	T		S	I	R
I	M	A	G	I	N	A	T	I	V	E
T	I	M	E	S		M	A	N	E	S
S	L	O	T	H		S	I	G	N	S

24

A	D	A	H		B	L	E	B
L	I	M	A		O	T	E	L	L	O
O	R	A	L	S	U	R	G	E	O	N
H	E	L	L	E	R		S	A	I	L
A	S	I		N	B	A		T	R	A
S	T	E	P		O	C	A	S	E	Y
			A	S	N	E	R			
A	R	E	N	A	S		B	A	L	E
G	A	S		B	T	W		M	A	R
A	C	T	S		R	E	N	O	W	N
S	E	E	E	Y	E	T	O	E	Y	E
P	R	E	V	U	E		A	B	E	S
	M	E	L	T		H	A	R	T	

179

SOLUTIONS

25

```
ARAM  ITALY
SAME  MAMIE
TRANSPLANT
EEN  HOLDS
PEALES  OEDS
   EEES  EXE
AMORS  EDDIE
RIN  HARI
ANAD  SITSAT
  TASSE  ELA
 TENNISBALL
 LANAS  TRIO
 CRYPT  USES
```

26

```
CHAPEL  CLE
SOLACE  PAID
SIERRA  OPIE
   TURNTAIL
OILY  NIA
CREPT  STOLI
HAVOC  EOSIN
SNIPE  IBEAM
  PLS  ESME
DATELINE
USER  DOTTED
PFCS  EILEEN
ETH  BREAKS
```

27

```
 SCOWL  SIFT
SOOTHE  ECUA
ABSCAM  LIMN
TET  TONE
BRAD  NISSAN
 REMAX  ABU
PRIMADONNAS
ANC  SENAT
DRAMAS  GASP
   RITT  COE
ILSA  ARARAT
TEEN  NIPUPS
SEED  DOOZY
```

28

```
BASEMEN  MAR
INTRUDE  ADO
COUNTYCOURT
EMCEES  AMOO
PICS  ASAIR
SAO  TUTTUTS
  EGGOS
UNCTION  LOP
BOEUF  CARL
ALLI  INAREA
NOISELESSLY
GAN  DIOCESE
IDE  TENONER
```

29

```
SPATS  SLAG
CARET  COMER
ANGLOSAXONS
LOY  ATM  REV
PUL  TAP  ARP
STEM  TESLA
  ALERT
ACMES  YUAN
PSI  AIL  PTA
OLD  FDA  WOT
NEEDLEPOINT
EERIE  SINCE
 PSST  ELDER
```

30

```
 FLAG  ALIS
ALEDO  RANCH
SOSAD  IDARE
ARB  OPS  LOW
NEO  TOT  ILA
ASSN  RAVELS
  ERTES
ISSUER  OLGA
PAK  PAT  EON
AMI  RYE  VAT
SPREE  SUITE
SLUES  SPEED
 ENCS  AIDE
```

31

```
DEP  ADS  SNA
ILE  DEN  TEN
SARALEE  REG
SIFT  SECEDE
ENEMY  HELL
DEC  SPRITES
  THERESA
ASPERSE  DCC
SHIM  FEDOR
EATERS  CRUE
AFC  EASTEND
NTH  ARA  STO
  DID  SSS
```

32

```
RITT  OEIL
ABOIL  HENNY
MENLO  ADDIN
 SEEIN  OTE
MAI  WASOF
ALLS  MORTAL
RULER  MAHAL
LIELOW  LEAD
 CASER  MAS
MST  INTRO
STOAT  EENIE
GAMMA  SOTTO
TRYA  SHOE
```

33

```
 SMIRCH  SEW
BEATOUT  UNH
UNNECESSARY
CONRAD  CRAY
KRIS  LIEGE
SAX  SNOOZES
  SETIN
SERAPHS  PAS
KCARS  SOME
EZRA  ACUTER
TEENYBOPPER
CMS  MADEIRA
HAT  ABASES
```

34

```
RECAP  EMMER
AMOUR  TIARA
MUNGO  ADDON
 SUDS  REST
BOER  EDIT
ERR  DAYBOOK
REV  USA  MAN
GOAHEAD  EKE
 TELL  PAYE
ODOR  THIS
RAINY  EQUIP
CURIA  FUROR
ABEAM  TEENY
```

35

```
LIFES  BRANS
INLET  CHLOE
MEARA  SEPIA
 SORE  OHSO
ISH  SOB  AEF
SOIT  SAGA
MANET  SANDP
 TRET  IDEA
FEH  KAY  OAK
ILER  MAAM
NIPAT  TREAD
ADAIR  EAGLE
LENNY  STAFF
```

36

```
 POPTAB  STE
TAPIOCA  EHS
IRONCURTAIN
VERT  ORARE
ONTO  GNEISS
STO  THEART
  FROST
 OGRESS  SAM
PROUST  ATME
ANTIC  POOR
PASTHISTORY
ATE  ILLEGAL
SET  CARREL
```

SOLUTIONS

37
```
U P R I S E S █ G M A
P R O M I S E █ R A T
D O U B L E A G E N T
A S S E T S █ E T U I
T E E D █ O N E A L █
E S D █ G O R I L L A
█ █ C O L I C █ █ █ █
E R E L O N G █ B A T
A I D A N █ J A D E █
R C M P █ O B I T E R
W H O S T H E B O S S
A I N █ E N T E N T E
X E D █ L O E S S E R
```

38
```
C R T █ T U P █ H A D
L I E █ R N A █ O N E
A L L █ A D S █ T N T
W E E N I E S █ H A H
█ █ G E N R E █ E R R
S P R E E S █ A B O █
A L A █ E T A █ D O N
N A P █ A M P E R E █
N T H █ S N O O D █ █
Y O W █ A D R E N A L
A N I █ R I O █ E R A
S I R █ E N S █ S I N
I C E █ E G O █ S A D
```

39
```
D E R █ J I G █ D O S
O V E █ A N O █ O R E
L E A █ B Q E █ U A L
A R D U O U S █ B C S
P L E N T I F U L L Y
S Y M S █ S A T E E N
█ █ A T T I R E D █ █
R U N O U T █ R E N O
E N D P R O D U C T S
H E W █ B R I S K E T
A S E █ I I N █ E S L
B C E █ N A G █ R T E
S O P █ E L O █ S S R
```

40
```
M A C A O █ H A D E S
A G A R S █ A B O R T
T O N A L █ S A U N A
█ A B O M B █ B E G █
B E D S █ P E A L █ █
U R I █ A G E L E S S
R I A L S █ N A C H O
G E N E S I S █ R O B
█ B E A T █ T O P S █
O V A █ S O P H S █ █
P I C A S █ E A S E L
A I O L I █ E N E M Y
L I N E N █ P E R S E
```

41
```
C O A L S █ M A M A S
A B B E Y █ A B O R T
T R A I L B L A Z E R
T I T █ P O T █ A N I
L E E █ H O E █ R A F
E N D S █ T S E T S E
█ █ E L L E R █ █ █ █
C O W P E A █ G A S H
A N A █ A C T █ L E U
I L L █ D E W █ L I D
M I L L I S E C O N D
A N I O N █ R O W E L
N E S T S █ P O S S E
```

42
```
M A S S █ T R O P E S
P L A T █ R A R E L Y
H A L O █ E N T A I L
█ T R I A D █ C O P █
A L I E N S █ E T H █
P A N █ G U T █ █ █ █
E Y E █ O R R █ D A Y
█ █ █ T E A █ I R E █
S P A █ C D R O M S █
T A N █ S H E E R █ █
A U N T I E █ M A L E
F L U I D S █ I M A M
F I L L E T █ T A B U
```

43
```
P L A S M A █ █ P E P
R I C H E S █ S L U E
O P E R A S █ T A R E
█ █ E L E V A T O R █
█ O L D S T E R █ █ █
G N U █ S A V A N T █
A T L A S █ L E M O N
D O U B T S █ O P T █
█ █ B E C A U S E █ █
F O R E W A R N █ █ █
I R I S █ R E C I P E
L E N S █ E N A M O R
L O G █ D A P P L E █
```

44
```
I M P █ L E A █ █ █ █
B A A █ E A R █ E T A
I N T E N T I O N A L
D A R E S █ A N G L E
E N O L █ S L U R █ █
M A N █ A T H E I S T
█ █ S A C H E T S █ █
S P A T T E R █ H R S
C L I O █ S H U L █ █
H E N N A █ L O O S E
W A T E R C O U R S E
A S S █ C U R █ N I P
█ █ H E D █ S A Y █ █
```

45
```
A B R A M █ T A S E R
M O O L A █ O H A R E
I L L E R █ G A N E F
G E L █ A A A █ F B I
O R E █ C B S █ R U N
█ O R C A S █ E A S E
█ █ C I S T E R N █ █
B R O S █ A L E C S █
L E A █ V I I █ I T D
O P S █ A N T █ S E E
N A T A L █ I N C A N
D I E G O █ S E A L S
E R R O R █ T E N S E
```

46
```
S P O O R █ M C D L T
T E P E E █ O R R I S
M A I N S Q U E E Z E
T K O █ E U S E █ █ █
█ N O W I S █ N A M █
█ E A S T E R E G G █
L E E T █ O C T O █ █
C A R Y G R A N T █ █
D N S █ N U B I A █ █
█ M E L O █ R I A █ █
E A R P I E R C I N G
P R O A S █ T E N T H
H A M A S █ S E E S A
```

47
```
W A F E R █ R I N S E
P L U M E █ I C I E R
M E R I T █ S E L E S
█ B R E A K B E A T █
S H E S █ L E E █ █ █
E E L █ H Y D R A S █
A I O L I █ I G I V E
█ S W A T A T █ R E S
█ █ P A C █ A C N E █
H I R O S H I M A █ █
A C O R N █ T A R S I
W A N T A █ L T G E N
K L I E G █ L E O N A
```

48
```
S O I L █ B S I D E S
U N C A █ A N N O Y S
R E A M █ G I G U E S
E I L E E N F O R D █
█ █ S H I F T █ █ █ █
E L P A S O █ S A N D
L A I █ █ █ █ C H O █
M A N A █ E N S E A L
█ █ T A L I A █ █ █ █
█ G I B S O N G I R L
L I G E T I █ G A N T
G N O S I S █ E G A D
S A R T R E █ D O S S
```

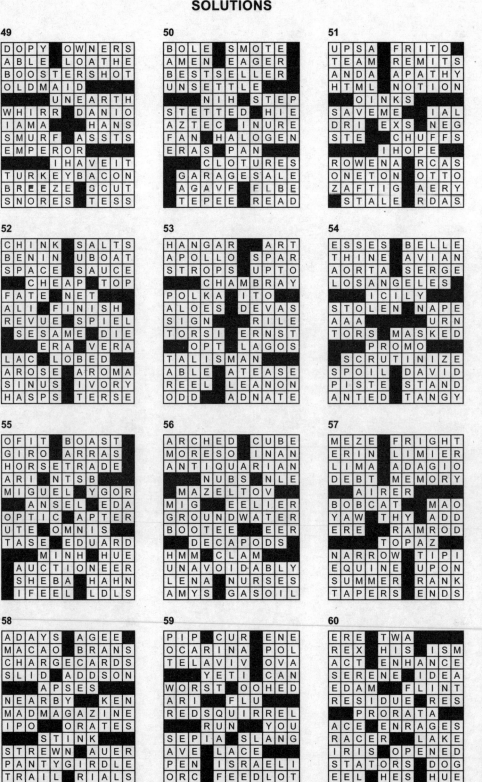

49

```
DOPY ■ OWNERS
ABLE ■ LOATHE
BOOSTERSHOT
OLDMAID ■ ■ ■
■ ■ ■ UNEARTH
WHIRR ■ DANIO
IAMA ■ ■ HANS
SMURF ■ ASSTS
EMPEROR ■ ■ ■
■ ■ IHAVEIT
TURKEYBACON
BREEZE ■ SCUT
SNORES ■ TESS
```

50

```
BOLE ■ SMOTE
AMEN ■ EAGER
BESTSELLER
UNSETTLE ■ ■
■ ■ NIH STEP
STETTED ■ HIE
AZTEC ■ INURE
FAN ■ HALOGEN
ERAS ■ PAN ■
■ ■ CLOTURES
GARAGESALE
AGAVE ■ FLBE
TEPEE ■ READ
```

51

```
UPSA ■ FRITO
TEAM ■ REMITS
ANDA ■ APATHY
HTML ■ NOTION
■ ■ OINKS ■ ■
SAVEME ■ IAL
DRI ■ EXS ■ NEG
STE ■ CHUFFS
■ ■ IHOPE ■ ■
ROWENA ■ RCAS
ONETON ■ OTTO
ZAFTIG ■ AERY
■ STALE ■ RDAS
```

52

```
CHINK ■ SALTS
BENIN ■ UBOAT
SPACE ■ SAUCE
■ CHEAP ■ TOP
FATE ■ NET ■ ■
ALI ■ FINISH
REVUE ■ SPIEL
■ SESAME ■ DIE
■ ERA ■ VERA
LAC ■ LOBED ■
AROSE ■ AROMA
SINUS ■ IVORY
HASPS ■ TERSE
```

53

```
HANGAR ■ ART
APOLLO ■ SPAR
STROPS ■ UPTO
■ ■ CHAMBRAY
POLKA ■ ITO ■
ALOES ■ DEVAS
SIGN ■ RILE
TORSI ■ ERNST
■ OPT ■ LAGOS
TALISMAN ■ ■
ABLE ■ ATEASE
REEL ■ LEANON
ODD ■ ADNATE
```

54

```
ESSES ■ BELLE
THINE ■ AVIAN
AORTA ■ SERGE
LOSANGELES
■ ■ ICILY ■ ■
STOLEN ■ NAPE
AAA ■ ■ URN
TORS ■ MASKED
■ ■ PROMO ■ ■
■ SCRUTINIZE
SPOIL ■ DAVID
PISTE ■ STAND
ANTED ■ TANGY
```

55

```
OFIT ■ BOAST
GIRO ■ ARRAS
HORSETRADE
ARI ■ NTSB ■
MIGUEL ■ YGOR
■ ANSEL ■ EDA
OPTIC ■ APTER
UTE ■ OMNIS ■
TASE ■ EDUARD
■ MINH ■ HUE
AUCTIONEER
SHEBA ■ HAHN
IFEEL ■ LDLS
```

56

```
ARCHED ■ CUBE
MORESO ■ INAN
ANTIQUARIAN
■ NUBS ■ NLE
■ MAZELTOV ■
MIG ■ EELIER
GROUNDWATER
BOOTEE ■ EER
■ DECAPODS ■
HMM ■ CLAM ■
UNAVOIDABLY
LENA ■ NURSES
AMYS ■ GASOIL
```

57

```
MEZE ■ FRIGHT
ERIN ■ LIMIER
LIMA ■ ADAGIO
DEBT ■ MEMORY
■ ■ AIRER ■ ■
BOBCAT ■ MAO
YAW ■ THY ■ ADD
ERE ■ RAMROD
■ ■ TOPAZ ■ ■
NARROW ■ TIPI
EQUINE ■ UPON
SUMMER ■ RANK
TAPERS ■ ENDS
```

58

```
ADAYS ■ AGEE
MACAO ■ BRANS
CHARGECARDS
SLID ■ ADDSON
■ ■ APSES ■ ■
NEARBY ■ KEN
MADMAGAZINE
IPO ■ ORATES
■ ■ STINK ■ ■
STREWN ■ AUER
PANTYGIRDLE
TRAIL ■ RIALS
■ ESTA ■ SAYST
```

59

```
PIP ■ CUR ■ ENE
OCARINA ■ POL
TELAVIV ■ OVA
■ YETI ■ CAN
WORST ■ OOHED
ARI ■ FLU ■ ■
REDSQUIRREL
■ RUN ■ YOU ■
SEPIA ■ SLANG
AVE ■ LACE ■ ■
PEN ■ ISRAELI
ORC ■ FEEDLOT
RYE ■ YAW ■ LSD
```

60

```
ERE ■ TWA ■ ■
REX ■ HIS ■ ISM
ACT ■ ENHANCE
SERENE ■ IDEA
EDAM ■ FLINT
RESIDUE ■ RES
■ ■ PRORATA ■
ACE ■ ENRAGES
RACER ■ LAKE
IRIS ■ OPENED
STATORS ■ DOG
EEL ■ HES ■ HUE
■ ■ MOT ■ ITS
```

61

```
L A G O _ R E C A P
E A R N _ I M B R U E
B L O O D V E S S E L
E T A _ R E N _ E R E
C O N C O R D _ N I C
_ L I A _ J I L T
_ M R E D _ B P O E
M E O W _ S E E
A R Y _ S U G G E S T
M C A _ M B E _ V E Y
B U L L E T T R A I N
O R W E L L _ E D N A
_ Y E N T E _ P E E N
```

62

```
R A P _ E E L _ A M P
A G E _ M A Y _ V I A
M E A S U R E M E N T
I N C H _ S A R E E
E T H I C S _ D A R N
_ R O P Y _ G A T
_ C A R R O U S E L
O R R _ D I L L
C O R P _ L E A S T S
T O A S T _ C A R T
A N N I E O A K L E Y
V E G _ S U N _ P A L
E R E _ T R Y _ A T E
```

63

```
_ S P A S M _ A D A S
C O A T E E _ K O F C
A N N E A L _ C A L E
N O I _ R E G _ T O N
A M C _ S E A B O A T
L A S S _ S N O U T S
_ T A C _ G E R
M A R R E D _ R O S S
A L I G N E D _ F A O
O K C _ O B O _ D L R
R A K E _ R E C U S E
I L E X _ I S H T A R
S I N E _ S T A Y S
```

64

```
A S P I C _ W A N D S
T I L D E _ I C E U P
E X A L T _ D E R M A
_ T E A S E _ V A N
S R I _ C A N T O
C A N O E D _ H U M P
U V U L A _ D O S E S
D E M I _ T R U S T S
_ B O G E Y _ Y E T
S O L _ E A S T S
A B O V E _ H O T E L
S O N E S _ O M E G A
H E D G E _ D E M O B
```

65

```
R A F T _ T U P E L O
O G R E _ E V A D E R
W A I L _ R U N O U T
A P E _ O S L O
N E D _ F E A R F U L
_ C O T _ S A L S A
S W A P _ M A A M
O A K U M _ L A G
U S E L E S S _ E B B
_ E N I D _ O R E
T E N N I S _ A L A S
E R I C A S _ L E V O
N A M E L Y _ A T O M
```

66

```
_ A C E _ S P A
R E S _ N A N _ H I P
H O T P O T A T O E S
O N A I R _ M O R S E
_ G S A _ O P T
S P E A K _ R E C T O
A R M _ H O W
N Y A L A _ G N A R L
_ N O R _ R A N
S P A I N _ A R G O N
M A G N I F I C E N T
O R E _ C A N _ D O H
G A R _ A N Y
```

67

```
C A D _ D R A P E S
A X I S _ E N T I R E
M E M O _ C A M E R A
P S E U D O
_ S L I M S _ E N E
B A T _ S P A _ N O R
E G O _ U R N _ J A G
E A R _ S E E _ O H S
P R E _ E S S A Y
_ S T R A T A
S A F A R I _ T B A R
A D A G I O _ S L I M
G O N E O N _ E L Y
```

68

```
D E B S _ A B A C U S
O R E L _ E T E R N E
O M N I P R E S E N T
W I D G E O N _ W A H
O N E O R _ S E I S
P E D _ I N F U L L
_ N O W A R
_ I C E D A M _ M S N
D S O S _ I P A N A
I S A _ A L S O R A N
P U R P L E H E A R T
S E S T E T _ M U L E
O D E S S A _ E D Y S
```

69

```
S O L E S _ S C A R E
O D I S T _ P U L E R
C O M P O S I T I O N
I N I _ G U T _ C I E
A T E _ I B E _ I L S
L O R R E S _ C A S T
_ A S T R A
S I M I _ A E R A T E
O N A _ D N S _ G O A
C C R _ A C E _ A M S
K I T C H E N E T T E
E T H E L _ D P H I L
T E A L S _ S T A T S
```

70

```
W O K _ I R E _ O D E
A P E _ C U T _ M I X
R E F R E S H M E N T
P R I E S T _ A L E E
S A R A H _ F R E O N
_ V E D A _ T U T
S C R E E N T E S T S
T A O _ T A C T
A V O W S _ H U M U S
M I T E _ M A D A M E
M A L T V I N E G A R
E R E _ A R C _ I M F
R E T _ T E E _ C I S
```

71

```
G O D S E N D
U P R I V E R _ T O G
S I A M E S E _ O W E
T U M _ T A L O N S
O M A H A _ D A T E S
_ S T A G E _ T H R O
_ I N E R T I A
S O C K _ R U N N Y
K R A I T _ T O D O S
I D L E R S _ N U T
E E L _ A L I B A B A
D R Y _ P A R R I E S
_ S T E A L T H
```

72

```
A N D E S _ A D D T O
S I R E E _ W O O E R
S T A R R _ O C U L I
N E W _ B O K _ B E N
S R I _ I L E _ L O O
_ N C A A _ D E S C
T A G O N _ F A C T O
E R S T _ N L E R
S I T _ G E O _ O A R
S S R _ R O T _ S S E
E T A P E _ S A S H A
R O W D Y _ A N E E D
A S S T S _ M A S S E
```

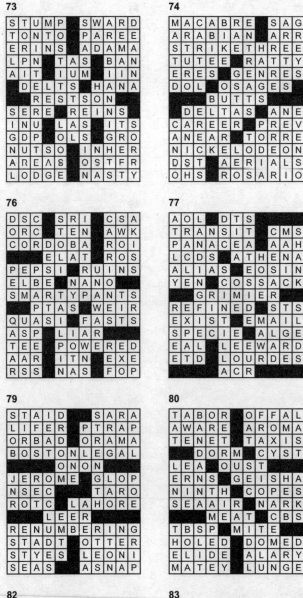

SOLUTIONS

73

S	T	U	M	P		S	W	A	R	D
T	O	N	T	O		P	A	R	E	E
E	R	I	N	S		A	D	A	M	A
L	P	N		T	A	S		B	A	N
A	I	T		I	U	M		I	I	N
	D	E	L	T	S		H	A	N	A
		R	E	S	T	S	O	N		
S	E	R	E		R	E	I	N	S	
I	N	U		L	A	S		I	T	S
G	D	P		O	L	S		G	R	O
N	U	T	S	O		I	N	H	E	R
A	R	E	A	S		O	S	T	F	R
L	O	D	G	E		N	A	S	T	Y

74

M	A	C	A	B	R	E		S	A	G
A	R	A	B	I	A	N		A	R	R
S	T	R	I	K	E	T	H	R	E	E
T	U	T	E	E		R	A	T	T	Y
E	R	E	S		G	E	N	R	E	S
D	O	L		O	S	A	G	E	S	
			B	U	T	T	S			
	D	E	L	T	A	S		A	N	E
C	A	R	E	E	R		P	R	E	V
A	N	E	A	R		T	O	R	R	E
N	I	C	K	E	L	O	D	E	O	N
D	S	T		A	E	R	I	A	L	S
O	H	S		R	O	S	A	R	I	O

75

R	E	B	A	G		A	C	K	E	E
P	R	O	M	O		M	A	N	L	Y
G	I	S	M	O		A	N	O	S	E
		T	O	P	D	R	A	W	E	R
C	F	O	S		E	A	R	L		
O	L	N		M	E	N	D	E	R	S
P	O	L		A	P	T		D	A	T
S	W	E	D	I	S	H		G	B	E
		T	O	T	E		T	E	E	N
I	N	T	E	R	A	L	I	A		
N	O	U	S	E		O	R	B	I	T
E	L	C	I	D		D	O	L	C	E
S	A	E	N	S		I	S	E	E	A

76

D	S	C		S	R	I		C	S	A
O	R	C		T	E	N		A	W	K
C	O	R	D	O	B	A		R	O	I
		E	L	A	T		R	O	S	
P	E	P	S	I		R	U	I	N	S
E	L	B	E		N	A	N	O		
S	M	A	R	T	Y	P	A	N	T	S
		P	T	A	S		W	E	I	R
Q	U	A	S	I		F	A	S	T	S
A	S	P		L	I	A	R			
T	E	E		P	O	W	E	R	E	D
A	A	R		I	T	N		E	X	E
R	S	S		N	A	S		F	O	P

77

A	O	L		D	T	S				
T	R	A	N	S	I	T		C	M	S
P	A	N	A	C	E	A		A	A	H
L	C	D	S		A	T	H	E	N	A
A	L	I	A	S		E	O	S	I	N
Y	E	N		C	O	S	S	A	C	K
		G	R	I	M	I	E	R		
R	E	F	I	N	E	D		S	T	S
E	X	I	S	T		E	M	A	I	L
S	P	E	C	I	E		A	L	G	E
E	A	L		L	E	E	W	A	R	D
E	T	D		L	O	U	R	D	E	S
				A	C	R				

78

C	O	P	R	A		O	S	I	E	R
F	E	T	A	S		C	O	N	D	O
C	R	A	S	H	L	A	N	D	E	D
			P	Y	A		A	O	N	E
S	E	T	S		Y	E	T			
O	U	R		A	R	R	A	N	G	E
P	R	O	G	R	E	S	S	I	O	N
H	O	T	S	E	A	T		N	O	V
		T	A	D		D	E	F	Y	
S	C	A	R		E	G	O			
C	O	M	I	C	R	E	L	I	E	F
A	R	E	N	A		N	O	O	N	E
M	A	N	G	Y		T	R	U	E	D

79

S	T	A	I	D		S	A	R	A	
L	I	F	E	R		P	T	R	A	P
O	R	B	A	D		O	R	A	M	A
B	O	S	T	O	N	L	E	G	A	L
	A	S	P		O	N	O	N		
J	E	R	O	M	E		G	L	O	P
N	S	E	C		T	A	R	O		
R	O	T	C		L	A	H	O	R	E
		L	E	E	R					
R	E	N	U	M	B	E	R	I	N	G
S	T	A	D	T		O	T	T	E	R
S	T	Y	E	S		L	E	O	N	I
S	E	A	S		A	S	N	A	P	

80

T	A	B	O	R		O	F	F	A	L
A	W	A	R	E		A	R	O	M	A
T	E	N	E	T		T	A	X	I	S
	D	O	R	M		C	Y	S	T	
L	E	A		O	U	S	T			
E	R	N	S		G	E	I	S	H	A
N	I	N	T	H		C	O	P	E	S
S	E	A	A	I	R		N	A	R	K
		M	E	A	T		C	B	S	
T	B	S	P		M	I	T	E		
H	O	L	E	D		D	O	M	E	D
E	L	I	D	E		A	L	A	R	Y
M	A	T	E	Y		L	U	N	G	E

81

S	E	G	E	R		A	L	E	D	O
O	S	A	G	E		D	I	C	E	D
R	O	T	O	G	R	A	V	U	R	E
A	L	O	T		O	R	I	A	N	A
			I	M	B	E	D			
P	H	A	S	E	I			I	D	E
C	O	N	T	I	N	E	N	T	A	L
S	D	S			H	I	E	I	N	G
		D	R	O	O	L				
E	M	B	R	Y	O		S	O	B	S
G	I	N	A	N	D	T	O	N	I	C
G	L	A	C	E		A	N	E	R	A
O	L	I	O	S		P	S	A	L	M

82

R	F	I	D		S	T	A	Y	U	P
E	I	N	E		P	A	N	A	M	A
G	R	A	S		A	R	A	R	A	T
I	S	M		A	S	T	A			
S	T	O	I	C		A	L	C	O	A
		R	N	S		R	I	A	T	A
A	B	A	T		C	R	T	S		
W	A	T	E	R		I	I	N		
E	R	A	S	E		M	A	I	Z	E
		T	E	M	P		V	O	A	
S	T	R	I	F	E		L	O	N	G
B	R	U	N	E	T		A	R	A	L
A	L	T	E	R	S		P	A	L	E

83

R	A	G	S		C	L	A	M	U	P
O	G	R	E		R	O	T	A	T	E
T	O	O	T		A	P	O	G	E	E
		S	T	A	M	E	N			
C	A	G	E	Y		R	A	M	S	
A	G	R	E	E		S	L	A	C	K
F	A	A						R	U	N
E	P	I	C	S		P	A	S	T	E
	E	N	O	L		A	B	U	S	E
		D	E	W	L	A	P			
Y	O	N	D	E	R		T	I	P	S
E	V	O	L	V	E		E	A	S	E
S	A	T	E	E	N		S	L	I	T

84

I	T	S	N	O		L	A	M	S	
N	E	N	E	S		N	I	P	A	T
B	E	A	U	T	I	F	U	L	L	Y
O	P	P		E	N	L		O	I	L
R	E	P	R	O	V	E		M	B	E
N	E	Y	O		I	R	A	B	U	
			I	C	O	S	A			
	S	I	S	A	L		R	O	D	E
L	O	N		M	A	K	E	M	A	D
U	S	D		E	T	A		E	R	I
C	O	U	N	T	E	R	P	A	R	T
R	O	C	C	O		M	A	R	I	E
E	N	T	R		A	H	A	N	D	

184

SOLUTIONS

85
BAR · SAC · ·
IPA · EGO · LAA
OPIATES · LAB
· SISS · GORE
ADELA · STYES
ADA · STAID · ·
AEF · IAL · BAA
· ANDRE · EAN
AIMEE · SINES
BRIC · CRIT · ·
BAL · TAOISTS
REY · ANO · EAP
· · BAM · NSA

86
USDT · RATTAT
RHEO · ENRAGE
DIAN · ANIMAL
UNTITLED · · ·
· HOOT · EELS
HAT · LYINGIN
EERIE · STOMA
FRACTAL · TOG
TYPE · DELI · ·
· · CLOSESET
MEMOIR · ETCH
EVOLVE · DIRE
TENDER · SCUM

87
ADZ · ABC · ANT
IRE · PRO · DOE
MAR · TOXEMIA
EPOS · KAKIS
RETAKE · ENOL
· ODIN · DIME
HAL · THY · SET
ALES · EAST · ·
SARI · AMORAL
· RAZOR · BALI
AMNESTY · TUN
DEC · LEO · OLD
ODE · ODD · RAY

88
CAB · AGE · TAP
USA · FAN · EVE
TSHIRTS · MAN
· NOEL · PIN
PANTS · APTLY
USER · OVA · ·
SHOULDERPAD
· DAD · TIDY
ASSET · SWEDE
THE · IDEA · ·
LAP · CALYPSO
ANI · ELM · APP
SKA · SEA · PAT

89
BOO · RDS · ABA
OEN · EEE · SOA
RIN · ENT · SLR
ALOHASTATE
· BREED · · ·
APRON · RARER
PAM · · COB
ESSES · SPANS
· ALANA · · ·
· PINACOLADA
AIS · VAR · BAN
RET · ERE · ADS
CDS · SIS · BEE

90
APSE · CASINO
PEAK · ORATOR
RACE · MOUSSE
ERR · SPUN · ·
SLIME · STOAT
· LEE · EERIE
EYES · · RARE
MAGMA · HEN
SKEET · EDGAR
· ROAR · ERA
GEMINI · BAIT
SEIZED · IDLE
ALTERS · NESS

01
SEGNO · COTES
TAROS · LOREN
IRONS · OHARE
GNU · USA · FIE
MEN · AUK · FEZ
ADDERS · DIRE
· CRYPTIC · ·
FLOE · ERECTS
RON · DNA · IAN
ANT · ODD · RYE
MERCY · UNCLE
ELOPE · COLOR
DYLAN · EWERS

92
TSARS · EGO
IMPALES · DEW
BEEFALO · INN
EAR · CBS · FOE
TRY · KOOKIER
· HEW · NESS
· ALONGSIDE
SNIP · RUT · ·
ADVISER · PRE
POE · TAM · RAM
PRO · ASININE
ERA · BESIEGE
DAK · ELDER

93
ARAB · TEASES
KOBE · IMBEAT
ITAL · RISQUE
OENO · ALE · ·
· DWAN · NCAR
ERO · LASCALA
LANAI · AESIR
SVELTER · SEE
AIDE · MAYA
· RPI · ENTR
HORTON · ADEE
STEELE · TRAM
ICEDAM · SAKS

94
· GNUS · WALLA
ARUSH · INAID
WORDOFMOUTH
NOSTRA · ANTE
EVE · NCO · DLR
DERM · ENTREE
· YELLOWY · ·
MESABI · ABOU
ATC · SFC · ACT
RAHM · TRISTE
BLOODSUCKER
LIONS · DUETO
EILAT · ESTS

95
FERRIS · KAE
RENEGE · DIMS
ONSALE · OLIO
· COMMUNAL
PHOTOLAB · ·
SANI · YELPED
IDIOM · SERBO
SINNED · GIAN
· TREELINE
BASILICA · ·
ODOM · COZIER
ADUE · ELEVEN
RLS · REDSEA

96
ARESO · SAGOS
CENTO · ARENT
TABOO · AROSE
OLLA · BERET
NEATH · SGTS
ERN · ARETES
· CARCASS · ·
· AENEAS · PIS
KITT · THANT
NENEH · OTHE
ILONA · DOTER
SLING · SHORE
HORAS · MANES

SOLUTIONS

97

```
B P S     K A R R A S
A R O W   I N E E D A
T A R A   S T E A D Y
S T E N T S
    L E A F Y   S E L
B O O   I R E   C D E
E D S   L O M   R A E
B E E   O M E   A N S
E R R   R A N U P
        R I B B O N
S A N G T O   I O N A
E M O T E S   D O N A
A S H O R E   K O N
```

98

```
P A P A S       E M S
A T R I U M   I M A C
S T E R N O   N O S H
T I L L   M A T T E L
A L A I   D E E R E
S A W N   H A R D U P
    E W E R S
A L E P H S   E G E R
R A D I O   C A V E
I M E L D A   T M E N
O E N O   F R I E N D
E N I T   I A O T S E
O T C   O N E O R
```

99

```
A L G A     A G A S
T H E R O D   D U L Y
H O O T I E   D A T S
  R E L I T   R A T
R I G   Y O K E D
E L E C   N O K I D S
T E C H S   S E A R S
S A L A A M   S N A G
  O T R A S   A G T
F L O   I M E A N
R E N T   A L I G H T
O D E R   S A T E E N
M A Y E   S L A I
```

100

```
H I D E   D O E S I N
A M E N   E S S E N E
L E T O F F S T E A M
A T A   L A I   S T E
L A T T I C E   A R S
    E E E   Z W E I
H A M E R   L O S E S
A T A N   I E R
R I T   A R B I T E R
P S I   W E E   A N A
I S L E O F C A P R I
S U D O K U   G A O L
T E A S E L   S S N S
```

101

```
G E N I C   P A C S
A B A S H   R E R U N
N O R M A   I F I D O
E L K   I T N   P S T
F I S H N E T   P I T
  A R T I C L E I
  G E R E   N L E R
F A N D A N G O
I B M   C O P Y C A T
N R A   T S R   E P I
N I S E I   E W E L L
Y E S N O   S A L U T
  L E A N   S L O S H
```

102

```
E B B S   M I A S M
G O A T   B O O B O O
O S L O   A R D E N T
S H A N G H A I
    L E A   S N A R F
S C A D S   S E N O R
A L I       T E A
Y I K E S   E G E S T
S P A N K   L A N
    S A C K R A C E
F A J I T A   A T O P
A M U L E T   G A P E
A P S E S   E L S E
```

103

```
O B I   D O N
C O N F I N E   P A R
A T T I R E D   R C A
    E V E N   B E R G
S A L E   I R I S E S
A I L   A G A T E
E R E   T H Y   N A B
  C L O T S   T I E
S E T U P S   D A M E
C R U X   T O O T
A N A   M A R T I A L
B E L   O N S H O R E
    A D O   N E T
```

104

```
D A F O E   S A B U
A V A S T   L A P E L
F A N F A R O N A D E
T N T   L O U D
  T A O I S T   W O W
  S T A Y S S A N E
R O T I       P T A S
F R I C A S S E E
D O C   T O T E R M
    Y A W P   L O C
I N T E R N E C I N E
R O S S I   T A N T E
A L A I   E P E E S
```

105

```
A D O B E       O M S
N E B U L A   C R I P
S I T S A T   O I S E
A C A I   O G L A L A
R E I N   S O N A R
A R N E   F O R A Y S
    S E U S S
B A L S A M   C T R S
I M A C S   H E E P
T O D A T E   E A T A
M U I R   L I M P I D
A R E D   O N E O N E
P S S   G S T A R
```

106

```
I B E T   M C D L
T O M S K   A P R E S
A B B E Y   R O U S E
S B A   R U T   N B A
C L R   A S I   K O L
A E R O   U N E A S Y
  A F F A I R S
H O S T E L   G A R B
O R S   N L E   S O A
N A M   C Y S   K O A
O T E R I   T H U M B
R E N I N   S O N I A
  S T A G   I K E A
```

107

```
B U L K S   H A W S E
A P P A L   O N E I S
M O N E Y O R D E R S
A N S   E R R S
    O S L O   P S Y
  I N T E R P O S E
R U D D     L E S H
S A L E S R O O M
A W E   P O R T
    T R U E   O S I
M I C H A E L J F O X
A S L A N   S O A M I
A P I N G   E N N E A
```

108

```
D A B   C A P   D A S
I R A   O B E   O N E
M I N D R E A D I N G
    A P T L Y
H O E R S   E K I N G
A R A C E   D E C A Y
N I S       A I R
K E Y E S   V O L V O
S L A T E   A R L E S
    A R E N A
D I S S E M I N A T E
E S O   N I T   C O D
M A N   E R Y   R E D
```

SOLUTIONS

109
```
C D S   S T E   E C T
O R A   A A S   M H O
P A R T Y P O O P E R
E N T E     S U R E R
  G O A T S   T E T E
    S M E E   S O S
  S L E E P L E S S
H E A   N A I L
E A T S   L E I L A
A L T E R     D O R A
R A I S O N D E T R E
E N C   M E N   T A R
R T E   A G A   A N O
```

110
```
M A C E S   S P A T S
I R O N Y   C O B R A
D A R E S S A L A A M
A B A   T A R   S I P
I L L   O R E   E L L
R E S U L T   E S S E
    L E O N E
P S S T   R E L I S H
R E M   T I E   N E O
E R A   W A D   T A U
F E R T I L I Z E R S
A N T E S   N O N C E
B E S E T   G O T H S
```

111
```
T A P   N B A   A M S
R A O   O R A   D U H
A U S S I E S   A S A
    T Y R A   A M E R
T H I N S K I N N E D
A U T O   I T T
R E S P O N S I B L E
      S O G   D L I X
S H R I M P T O A S T
L E A S   O A T S
E A N   D I N E T T E
E R I   O N I   E R N
K A N   A T A   D E C
```

112
```
R E B U S   U S A G E
A M I N E   F U S E D
F U N C T I O N I N G
    L A N   B A T E
D O S E   V I E
E D O   B E R A T E D
M I R R O R I M A G E
I N T E R N S   K I N
    T E E   F A S T
O F F S   S O L
P L A I N S P O K E N
T O N N E   A R E N A
S W E A T   H A N D Y
```

113
```
R A T S O   P I Q U E
E L E N A   S T U P E
M A L E S   A S I A N
O N E L   P L I E
    G L E A M   T A B
B U R S A R   A N E
A S A   T A D   S E M
L I P   S E W A G E
M A H   R O R E M
    W E A L   T O G S
A L I B I   A B U S E
L I R A S   M A S O N
A L E N E   C R E S S
```

114
```
N I T T I   E G G E D
E V I A N   D U A N E
Z O R R O   O N L O W
    E N U F   G A L S
L E S   R A M A
A V O W   S E D A T E
G A M E R   N I V E N
O N E S E C   N E R D
    T E A K   M N O
R O H E   D I D A
O L O R D   T O R O S
M E R L E   T R I E S
E A S Y A   Y E A R S
```

115
```
S E P T I C   S O I L
A S I A G O   O N M E
D A N S O N   V E N A
  G E T S R I D O F
L A P   O U S E
O B O   M S T A R S
E R N   G E S   D E E
B I G S U R   H I S
  M A G I   E N E
S C L E R O S I S
P O O L   O N H I R E
E C C L   D O O V E R
C A K Y   S T P E T E
```

116
```
P I C O T   I N M E
O M A R R   N E A T H
T A N G O   D O N H O
P G A   M O R N I N G
I E D   P E A   F I G
E D I T E D   P E C S
    A U D   S A S
E S N E   A C C T N O
A P B   E P H   A A A
G R A N D A M   T I T
L U C I D   U T I L E
E C O L I   C H O I R
  E N S E   K E N T S
```

117
```
S A B R A     A S Y E
A G E O L D   H T M L
W A S A B I   A A H S
    I D E A S   N A E
P A D   E L C I D
U S E E   S A L I N E
T H O N G   N Y N E X
S E N O R S   A G R O
    E L E N A   G O D
A D S   G I N S U
G E E K   P O T A S H
H A L E   E D E R L E
A R F S   E N D O W
```

118
```
A M A H   I M A G E
R E L I C   B A N E S
A D I E U   I R O N S
B I G   R O S E T T E
S A N S E I   H E N
    P A L E   E E C
W H E A L   M E R L E
O A R   L O B E
O V A   P A L A C E
D E S E R T S   S E A
M A U V E   S H I R R
A G R E E   Y O D E L
N O E N D   T E D S
```

119
```
G A S P E   B A S T
A N W A R   A B O R C
R E E C E   L E C A R
A M E S   R E T I N A
N I T   A A S   A C T
D A T O N G   E L E E
    E D I T O R S
S A M S   I N A C A B
P U P   B M I   I P O
O N E S I E   R E P O
O T R A S   L I N E D
L I E T O   V O C A L
  E D A N   I S E R E
```

120
```
A N D N O   E M E R Y
M O R E L   S A D I E
S W I M S   T H I G H
O I L B E A R I N G
    L U N G E
D E B T   R E D T O P
U M I A K   T O O L E
O U T L A Y   G L A D
    R U E H L
  D O N A L L O G U E
S A J A K   L U A N N
S H A M U   A S T O N
E L I E L   S E E S A
```

121

```
S R I S . . I C U S .
T O N E R . C A N A L
R A T I O . E D I L E
I R R . A M C . N O T
K A A . D O O . T O T
E T N A . O L S E N S
. . S T A N D I N . .
S N I V E L . E T C H
C O G . R I D . I O U
A R E . O T E . O H M
B O N U S . A P N E A
S O C K O . L E A R N
. M E R L . G L E E .
```

122

```
A M B O . . C A P O S
R E I N . B O L I D E
E R G O . I R I T I S
N I B . A T E . C O T
A N A . R E D . H U E
S O N N E T . T E S T
. . G O A H E A D . .
A C T S . E D I B L E
D O H . A D D . A I D
O R E . B U Y . T A U
B O O T H S . O T I C
E N R O O T . E L S F
S A Y E R . . R E E D
```

123

```
A S C O T . C H A R T
F O R T E . P U R E E
F L U T E . A G A T E
O D I O U S . O B I T
R E S . P U P . I R E
D R E G . S O C C E R
. . C A P T I O N . .
P H O B I A . B U R G
I O N . T I C . M A R
R O T H . N O V E N A
A P R I L . P E R K S
C L O N E . R I A L S
Y A L T A . A L L E Y
```

124

```
B U I L D . A L F A S
I N O U R . M A R L A
R I N S O . A T A L L
R A I . P J S . P E I
S T A P L E S . P A N
. S E W . F E R E . .
. T A S T E L E S S .
C O L T . L E A . . .
R S S . T E A R G A S
A P O . O R K . I B E
D A R B S . A M B E R
B R A H E . G A B L E
Y E N T A . E L S E S
```

125

```
. R A C E . S O L E .
S E R R A . M A A M S
T H A T S B E T T E R
O A R . Y U L . E R A
P B A . O Y L . L I S
A S T I N . I D Y L .
. . I T S N O . . . .
. M I N H . G I D D Y
D O N . E E S . E R E
A N S . E X A . A I N
D A I L Y P L A N E T
E D D I E . T E N S E
. S E I S . S C A T .
```

126

```
H E B . K D S . P O L
A M I . E A T . R E M
M I N T E D I T I O N
. . . E P O N Y M . .
D A L L A S G R E E N
O D I S T . S A C R E
Y A N . . . . U N M .
O M E G A . C A T I E
U N D E R T H E S E A
. . R E N O I R . . .
K A I S E R R O L L S
A I V . T S R . E G O
S A E . T O S . R E D
```

127

```
M I C . O S O . . . .
A L A S K A N . S E A
L I N E A T E . W E S
T A T E . U R G E N T
A C H I E R . T A S E
. . E N I D . S T I R
D C C . N A M . B E S
E L O I . Y A L U . .
R A M S . N A I L E D
M U E S L I . M L L E
A D D . U G L I E S T
L E Y . S H A T T E R
. . H T C . S S E . .
```

128

```
O L M O S . M E T A L
F O E H N . G A R N I
F I R E A N D R A I N
. . I D I O . L Y L E
L O D . L A N G . . .
E R I C . M A R S H A
S W A R M . P E P Y S
S E N O R S . Y E P S
. . S T E N . L E N .
A F B S . R I L L . .
P E R E S T R O I K A
S E E Y A . O M N I A
E S T E S . S E G A R
```

129

```
G A S . C S S . S A P
O B E . O T O . T D S
O I L L A M P . I I S
F E L I X T H E C A T
. . E E E . I N K . .
A U R A S . A V I A N
N T S B . . . E N Y O
S A M O S . A N G S T
. . A V A . B O P . .
F O R E V E R M O R E
A C K . E R O S I O N
C H E . M E A . N U N
T O T . E S D . T E A
```

130

```
C A S A S . B O C C I
I N A N E . U B O A T
R A N D A . T O W N E
. . T E N E T . L A R
B E A S . A R T . . .
A V A . S L E U T H .
N A N C E . S A V O R
. H A R A S S . C U E
. . I M P . M A R E .
C W M . L A R A M . .
O R A T E . O N E A D
C A R R S . T E R R E
A Y R E S . I T A G O
```

131

```
A M M O . . L A U D .
S E A R S . A N N E X
S A C R A . C A I N E
E L K . G A T . T U N
T I E . E R E . E D O
S E R A . S A D D E N
. . E C H E L O N . .
S U L T A N . C A T S
H R S . B I B . T H E
R A H . I C E . I R E
U N A P T . S L O O P
B U R S A . T O N N E
. S K I T . U S E D .
```

132

```
L A C . S P A . T A P
E L A S T I C . A L A
K E R O U A C . N O N
. . T O P F L I G H T
O P I N E . A S S A Y
A R E . . . A I L . .
F O R G E T M E N O T
. . . E N E . A W E .
B R A N D . S M I L E
L E I T M O T I V . .
O T T . O N E S E L F
O R C . S C A T T E D
D O H . T E L . Y E A
```

SOLUTIONS

133
```
SAY BRO STY
ICE REV KOI
RESTITUTION
   ICILY
SAFEKEEPING
CLASS SEDER
ALI     IRE
LINKS STOVE
ANTICIPATED
   TONER
ALTERCATION
PEA CUR TWO
TIN HRS SET
```

134
```
MIRA ABATE
ONES LIGER
TURPENTINE
IRA  YIELD
FENNEC ERAS
  BLOC ILO
FORCE HULAS
EVA  TSAR
YAWS ORNATE
  DEALT DEL
TENNISBALL
EASED UGLI
CLEWS MESS
```

135
```
ENDED CEASE
BEENA WALES
BLOODSTREAM
   KOO LESE
SANI  USD
INA OTTOMAN
MISSTHEMARK
SLITHER ING
  REA BLOB
ALDA  SHE
PAINSTAKING
OINGO RANAT
CREED EATNO
```

136
```
SWOPS ELMS
NAURU REACT
ENTERTAINER
ETA LOS GNU
ZAG YOU LEE
EDEN TREES
  ASHEN
NONOS DESK
SAN MOP TAI
OPS EMS HUN
FAIRHEARING
ALTHO LOCAL
MEOW MESSY
```

137
```
LAP ACE BOB
UZI PASSEUL
CONTEMPLATE
AINU  YUCCA
SCARAB THOR
  BRUT EMS
 RIOGRANDE
TEC OKRA
OVEN ATTACK
RECUR AGUE
PROBABILITY
OILSKIN LIE
RED ENS END
```

138
```
KUDOS BALDS
ASIDE AFOOT
TENET STONE
ADO BET PEP
  SUAVER
FIANCE OILS
CLUCK MANIA
CORA FISTED
  PALATE
ORB BUS GOY
ROOMY MERGE
CORPS ATALL
STAGS SHLEP
```

139
```
SAB PIT
AGE STUCCOS
DOWNTOEARTH
ARIOSO NEER
TALK OTARU
EDITED MIG
 EASEOFF
BAR AENEID
RUMOR YLEM
UTEP PAELLA
CONANOBRIEN
ESTHETE NAE
   USD GDS
```

140
```
UNC PAS DAS
SAL TRITONE
DRAWERLINER
TAMAR KEATS
  PROSIT
GTE TEABAG
NOTYOURCALL
POTEEN NGO
  NUTMEG
MADTV CLIMB
SQUAREDANCE
RUSSELL TCB
PIK SGT OVE
```

141
```
WASAT GHIA
ALERO RUNAT
RADAR INDRA
HMO RDS IGN
EON EIS VHS
ADAS AOKI
DEARE MIDAS
  ROXY AUNT
ORI PDS ATE
PEZ ASA LOI
ALOAN LAING
LINUS SUZIE
CAKE AREAR
```

142
```
POPPA ASHER
ARIEL SPARE
NEEDLEPOINT
SODA VEILED
  GNARL
SALOON SAT
PROGRESSIVE
ACT SETTEE
  PACER
SESAME ETNA
TREPIDATION
AIRES SCENE
BEARS SHREW
```

143
```
ATALOSS
LUNATIC BEG
PLANTAR ARE
HIT MACRON
APHID PARSE
 SEBUM BEES
 MINIMAL
SPAS DONOR
NOTED BARED
ARISEN GNU
FEZ COPLAND
USE ALIENEE
  LOCUSTS
```

144
```
RST LAC
APO ACH FDS
NAUTICA REA
ESTH UPSELL
EMERIL LETO
  NAST AZAN
VISCOUNTESS
ONEI RETD
IRMA APERCU
COBNUT RYAN
EAL FINNISH
DDE OOF NEA
   SNL GST
```

SOLUTIONS

145

```
S E L L _ _ O B O L
A L O E S _ N E R O S
D O U B L E E A G L E
H I D _ R X S _ A L I
U S E _ S I T I N O N
S E R B _ S A R A P E
_ _ A S T R O _ _ _
S E D U C E _ B M O C
H E R M A N N _ I R A
I L E _ R C A _ Z I N
M I D D L E S I Z E D
S E G U E _ A D E N O
_ R E G T _ I N T R
```

146

```
M O N S _ A M P L Y
A R E A S _ P U R E E
C I R C A _ A M I G O
R E V _ N B C _ M A M
O N O _ D O H _ A T E
S T U B _ N E U R O N
_ _ S A T I S F Y _ _
U P S H O T _ O C A S
P L Y _ P O I _ O W L
R E S _ L S D _ L A Y
O U T R E _ E V O K E
O R E O S _ A I R E S
T A M E S _ I S N T
```

147

```
C O I N S _ S A G A
E N N U I _ B I K E R
P E N A L _ A B A T E
_ _ K N O T T Y _ _
O P E C _ E C L A T S
C H E E T A H _ C O T
T O P _ U T E _ C R U
A T E _ M I S L E A D
D O R S U M _ A S H Y
_ _ P L E A T S _ _
N E H R U _ R E I G N
A R I E S _ E L O P E
B A S E _ S Y N O D
```

148

```
R A N D _ H A L E D
O L E N _ M O N E T A
P L E A B A R G A I N
E S D _ E P A _ R E I
D O S S E L S _ N N E
_ _ O N E _ K E N L
C A M U S _ T A R E S
A L O P _ M E A _ _
S U I _ C A N T A T A
A M S _ U S S _ C Y S
B I T E T H E D U S T
A N E M I A _ A R O O
S A N T E _ T E N N
```

149

```
M E D A L _ S H I N E
A L I K E _ P E C A N
S I D E B _ A R O M A
_ M I L E S T O N E _
_ _ A C T I I _ _
O L E S _ R A N S O M
A I S _ N U L _ K G S
S A L T E D _ M A S S
_ _ O T E R O _ _
_ S M A L L A R M S _
S E E T O _ H A H A S
O R L E S _ A L O N E
D E L E S _ B E S E T
```

150

```
E R L E _ L A T E N T
N E A L _ O R A T O R
C A K E S A N D A L E
E R E C T _ E S S A Y
_ _ T O L L _ _
C A M E R A _ C A G E
S C R E E N S A V E R
A C I S _ D E R I D E
_ _ D O R Y _ _
A B B I E _ T A M L A
C O O P E R A T I O N
A L L U R E _ I L R C
D O T T E D _ D A I S
```

151

```
S P T _ P T S
I L A _ I O S _ S H H
R E B _ T R A C H E A
I N L A T E _ C O L D
U T E P _ O R R I N
S Y M P T O M _ T O T
_ A L U M N U S _
O L N _ R A I S I N S
B E N I N _ O G L E
E D E N _ D A S H E R
S U R G E O N _ T A V
E P S _ B E D _ E S E
_ W R Y _ D T S
```

152

```
B A C H _ H A R A S S
A S H Y _ A R A B I A
L E A D _ R E B O R N
L A I R _ D A B
_ R A K E _ I S M S
S I L T I N G _ P E T
I C I E R _ O B E S E
O A F _ K N E E C A P
N O T E _ A S C I
_ _ M O T _ L A D S
W A P I T I _ O L I O
O P O R T O _ U L N A
N E L S O N _ D Y E R
```

153

```
P I C S _ T R A D E R
A C H E _ R E V I V E
D E A D _ E V A D E D
_ _ P A C K E T _ _
S W A T H _ R A D S
K O R E A _ B R A W L
E R R _ _ L O U
W R A P S _ S P A R K
_ Y L E M _ K L I N E
_ _ S O C I A L _ _
E U R E K A _ N A P E
G R A T E R _ E M I R
O N W A R D _ T A P E
```

154

```
A P P T _ H A S A T
B L E E P _ O F U S E
B A N T U _ M O N T E
A N T _ L E E R S A T
S T A B L E R _ H R H
_ G A U S S _ I T E
T R O M P _ I N N E D
R O N _ S O M M E _
U S B _ T A P E S U P
C A R C A S S _ T R A
K N A C K _ O N A I R
E N S U E _ N O T E S
R A S P S _ D E L I
```

155

```
N A S A L _ O W I E
A A H E D _ A B E A M
I R O N S _ H O L T S
R E V E _ T O L L
_ E I G H T _ Q B S
F O L D E R _ U R E
I D I _ T O O _ A E R
L E N _ A K E L A S
L A G _ S T A S I
_ S P R Y _ P F C S
P O N T A _ D A I L Y
A L O E S _ O N E O F
M A W R _ C A D D Y
```

156

```
T O P O S _ S T O A
A W A S H _ G H O U L
X E N I A _ A R O S E
I N T E R S T A T E
_ _ R I P E N _ _
A G E S _ O A K L E Y
S A W _ G N U _ E R E
S P E A R S _ P E A T
_ _ N A O M I _ _
_ C O N T R O L L E D
D U B A I _ C L O S E
A R I L S _ H A U S A
B E T S _ A R D E N
```

157

```
D U A D S ■ G E R M S
A Z U R E ■ O X E Y E
L I T U P ■ D E M O N
■ O B I S ■ S O P S ■
R A M ■ A I R ■ T E E
A W A Y ■ P O R E ■ ■
F E T E S ■ B O C C E
■ I S L E ■ T O O L ■
S A C ■ Y A P ■ N O D
C R A B ■ T E S T ■ ■
A G L O W ■ T O R S I
D O L L Y ■ A L O O F
S T Y L E ■ L O L L S
```

158

```
K L A N ■ K E N T S
N A D A ■ H E U R E
I N M E ■ R A N C O R
C D I ■ T E N ■ L Y E
K A N ■ H A S B E E N
S U I T E D ■ R A R A
■ S A N D B A R ■
N A T L ■ R E C E S S
A D R A T E S ■ N T H
C H A ■ A S S ■ E R A
R E T O S S ■ P R E P
E R O S E ■ A G E E
S E R F S ■ N Y P D
```

159

```
E G B D F ■ B A N D O
S A R D I ■ A L E A N
P R E E X I S T E N T
I G A ■ T R I ■ D I I
E L S ■ U A L ■ T E M
D E T E R S ■ I O L E
■ D E C A F ■
P C P S ■ I S A A C S
U L E ■ R B H ■ S H E
T I T ■ E L A ■ S O N
S Q U A R E M E A L S
C U L P A ■ E D I L E
H E A R N ■ D A L A I
```

160

```
P A G E S ■ I D L E
E L R O Y ■ G L O A M
L O E S S ■ E L U T E
O T E ■ C P R ■ B R R
S O N ■ O R U ■ L I I
I F H E ■ A N N E A L
■ O N E I D A S ■
C O U G A R ■ W A S P
R S S ■ R I G ■ W A R
A C E ■ W E L ■ B Y O
M A G N I ■ E T U I S
B R A G G ■ A B C D E
O S S O ■ M A K O S
```

161

```
K A P U T ■ S T R E W
N O R M A ■ T H E T A
I N E P T ■ R E P A Y
T E C ■ T R U E R ■
■ I S L E T ■ O A T
E L O P E D ■ D A N E
P O U R S ■ C O C O A
E A S Y ■ A L O H A S
E N S ■ S C A R F ■
■ T O T E M ■ U S A
A B O V E ■ O R L O N
C A N E R ■ R E L I T
T H E R E ■ S T Y L E
```

162

```
A L F A S ■ F I S T S
L E O N E ■ A S P I C
E E R I E ■ N A I R A
■ S T O P S ■ I T E M
S H U N ■ M O A T ■
C O N ■ S O P H I S M
A R E ■ Y O U ■ N E O
R E C A N T S ■ G N U
■ O U C H ■ C I T E
S C O T ■ S W A M I
O A K U M ■ O R A N G
P R I M E ■ W A G E S
S P E N T ■ S T E L A
```

163

```
N A P A ■ C A C T I
I N A L L ■ O V O I D
B A R G E B O A R D S
■ R A G A ■ I R E ■
O H O ■ A G I L E ■
G E T ■ L A N ■ S H E
R A F ■ E T H ■ P A P
E R A ■ S E A ■ O R E
■ S M E L L ■ N E E
■ C H A ■ L A U D ■
C H I C K E N F E E D
P O O L E ■ T O N G A
A P N E A ■ S T O W
```

164

```
A C T V ■ S H I N T O
B A R I ■ N I N E O F
E R I E ■ O T T A W A
L E G W A R M E R S
■ E S K E R ■
S H A D E S ■ N I C K
L I D ■ T O E
A P E D ■ C I N E M A
■ A A L T O ■
■ H U D S O N H A W K
T A N G O S ■ E R E I
A T T U N E ■ L O A N
I S O M E R ■ P O N G
```

165

```
A M A J ■ B R A S S Y
R A Z E ■ R U S H A T
A T U S ■ O B T U N D
T H R U W A Y ■
■ E C S T A S Y
R A D I S H ■ M L L E
I N E R T ■ G A M U T
S K E E ■ M O N A M I
C A R S E A T ■
■ V R O O M E D
B I O P I C ■ R E D O
C A L I C O ■ C L I P
S T E N T S ■ H O N E
```

166

```
B A S I C ■ A D E A D
D I T K A ■ B O F F O
A D R E P ■ I N F O R
Y E A ■ S W E ■ L U M
S S I ■ T A S ■ O L A
■ G L A D ■ A R O N
C O H A N ■ C L E F T
H U T T ■ M O E S
A T F ■ O M M ■ C W M
U V A ■ R I P ■ E R Y
C O C O A ■ O M N I S
E T E X T ■ R E C T O
R E D Y E ■ T W E E N
```

167

```
K A S E M ■ R E I D S
E L E N I ■ O R N O T
M E L O N ■ D E T R E
A T F ■ I D E ■ H I V
L A C ■ B Y O ■ E T E
■ O P U S ■ A S O N
S I N U S ■ C L A S S
H O F F ■ P A L M
E N E ■ T E N ■ E R A
G E S ■ H U D ■ V O L
O S S I E ■ I G E T A
A C E T O ■ E R I C S
T O D O S ■ D U N S T
```

168

```
T A L K S ■ A C T O
U N I A T ■ R H I N O
N O V I A ■ E A T E N
E X E ■ B E W I T C H
D I S A B L E ■ L A O
■ A F L E A ■ C E R T
■ O L D S A L T ■
S S R S ■ T R E A S
T O T ■ R I S O T T O
P R O D U C E ■ T R W
A R D E N ■ N O L I E
T E A M O ■ I M E A N
■ L Y O N ■ C E D E S
```

SOLUTIONS

169

```
SHE ALP PAR
OAR SARDINE
FLASHPOINTS
TOSH   PAW
  ASP SHMO
 BOWTIE EAR
COMMANDMENT
RON BODILY
TRIG NYC
 VOW RAFT
AGORAPHOBIA
FORESEE ERR
TOE HAM TEE
```

170

```
ARMOR CIGAR
AMADO HURTS
ANNAS IMACS
 ASSAD HOS
COG IRENA
EXEUNT AMON
PESCI SICKO
ENOL ALFRED
 MAUNA ADE
GBE DESAC
LAHTI HIKES
UCONN EDEN3
TOWNE RARER
```

171

```
GAMEY PILOT
ADAGE ALIBI
GANGS ELFIN
ERIN CASE
 FOEHN PRO
GEEGEE RAP
HAS LAP ERA
EST TASSEL
ETA EERIE
 TSAR ERRS
TRIOS ANVIL
ANODE ANELE
BANAL HARED
```

172

```
HEAT CANCAN
ALLI OTOOLE
IMAGINATIVE
GOWEST ANAD
 HONK
WERE REEFER
PLANETARIUM
MOWGLI SSRS
 AKON
TWIG NABORS
HISEMINENGF
EMMIES HEMP
OPENIT RCPT
```

173

```
ESSEN AEC
ALEXIE SALE
SCRIMP URLS
 TEENBEAT
 POSSESS
BEST SEESAW
OPART CREPE
SAYAAH VLAD
 TRIVIAL
ABSENTEE
ROEG MENACE
ARAY ECCLES
GAM KEANE
```